## Praise for *Jumping into the Parade*

A real-life story of redemption, *Jumping into the Parade* is a call to action for us all to live our lives more consciously. Every reader will learn something from this book.

> —KEN BLANCHARD, coauthor of *The One Minute Manager* and *Lead Like Jesus*

You won't find many authors as vulnerable, forthright, and real as Tim Brown. This book teaches us that we are all broken and beautiful—and the only way to find true joy and love is to put all our eggs in our "Faith, Family, and Friends" basket.

> —TOMMY SPAULDING, *New York Times* bestselling author of *It's Not Just Who You Know*

*Jumping into the Parade* is a powerful read. The words, stories, and language used in this book are evolutionary in nature. From my view, it is rare for a business leader of Tim Brown's caliber to throw down the gauntlet on the truth. This book is real, and the lessons are liberating on every level, for anyone interested in living a more powerful and authentic life.

> —STEPHEN McGHEE, visionary leadership guide and author of *Get Real: A Vital Breakthrough on Your Life and Leadership*

Tim Brown's book should be recommended reading for everyone, but particularly for those who are at a crossroads in life when the next steps they will take are so critical. Coming to grips with the unaddressed questions in life is something we all have in common. Tim masterfully guides us toward greater fulfillment through his own story of triumph.

—PHILIP ANSCHUTZ, the Anschutz Corporation

I have had the pleasure of knowing Tim Brown for many years. Reading *Jumping into the Parade* reminded me of how often our masks keep us from really knowing what our friends are struggling with, while we often are hiding our own struggles from them. Tim's vulnerability gave me a deeper appreciation for the man he is, and served as an encouragement for me to be more real and open in my own relationships. In *Jumping into the Parade*, Tim shares his journey from despair to fulfillment and gives practical steps that we can take in our own lives to evaluate where we are headed, and maybe, how to get to a better place. We probably have all had times when we felt like Tim did in that elevator. I'm glad Tim pushed the "down" button!

—DR. BOB BELTZ, Sr. Pastor, Highline Community Church, Denver

# JUMPING INTO THE PARADE

# JUMPING INTO THE PARADE

## THE LEAP *of* FAITH *That* MADE
## MY BROKEN LIFE WORTH LIVING

BY TIM BROWN

*Foreword by Bob Buford*

BenBella Books, Inc.
Dallas, Texas

BenBella Books, Inc.
10300 N. Central Expressway
Suite #530
Dallas, TX 75231
www.benbellabooks.com
Send feedback to feedback@benbellabooks.com

Printed in the United States of America
10  9  8  7  6  5  4  3  2  1

Library of Congress Cataloging-in-Publication Data:
Brown, Tim (Executive)
   Jumping into the parade : the leap of faith that made my broken life worth living / by Tim Brown.
      pages   cm
   Includes bibliographical references and index.
   ISBN 978-1-940363-33-2 (trade cloth : alk. paper) — ISBN 978-1-940363-48-6 (electronic)   1. Brown, Tim (Executive)   2. Converts—Colorado—Biography.   3. Life change events—Religious aspects—Christianity.   4. Christian life—Colorado.   I. Title.
   BV4935.B76A3 2014
   277.3'083092—dc23
   [B]
                                                    2014016423

Editing by Debbie Harmsen
Copyediting by James Fraleigh
Proofreading by Michael Fedison
   and Rainbow Graphics
Cover design by Connie Gabbert

Text design and composition by
   Publishers' Design and Production
   Services, Inc.
Printed by Lake Book Manufactur-
   ing, Inc., Melrose Park, IL

Distributed by Perseus Distribution: www.perseusdistribution.com

To place orders through Perseus Distribution:
Tel: (800) 343-4499
Fax: (800) 351-5073
E-mail: orderentry@perseusbooks.com

Significant discounts for bulk sales are available. Please contact
Glenn Yeffeth at glenn@benbellabooks.com or (214) 750-3628.

*To my son,*

*May you live every second of every day in the full knowledge of God's unconditional love for you. Cherish the blessing of your life. Don't take anyone or anything for granted. Be true to your "Self" and you will always be filled with peace, joy, and clarity of your purpose.*

*Love,*

*Dad*

# Contents

# Foreword

IT WOULD BE NICE to tell you that Tim Brown's story is unique—that no one has ever gone through the types of trials and experiences that took him, quite literally, to the edge of death. It would be nice to tell you that this is a great read (it is) and an interesting story (it is), but that the rest of us need never worry about going there ourselves.

In a way, that's true. But in a much more important way, it's not.

That's one of the beauties of our humanity. We're all different. We all go through life on a path that's unique to our upbringing, our relationships, our DNA, our work experiences, our . . . well, our everything.

But as humans, we all share some common threads. We might like different types of movies, but we all like to be entertained. We all want to be loved. We all want to be accepted. We all want to feel respected, to feel valued. We all feel lost at times. We all get disillusioned. We all want to find our purpose and have meaning in our lives. And we all hurt when life doesn't go as we would like it to go.

These threads bind us together and allow us to relate to each other and learn from each other. They give us empathy for other people, and they help us draw parallels to our own lives.

When I read Tim's touching and amazingly transparent story, I realized at once that he's traveling on a unique and fascinating journey, but that many of the pitfalls, emotions, and trials of his life are common to men and women all over the world, especially those (of us) who've pushed hard for success in the first half of our lives.

I get emails almost daily from and about people who look to all the world like they've never made a mistake in life. They have nice homes, high-paying jobs, and a Hallmark-picture-perfect family. Everything they touch seems to turn to gold. But the outside world sees only the surface; on the inside, there are problems—affairs, addictions, depression, greed, loneliness, pride, insecurities . . .

Tim isn't an island, and there's comfort for him in that fact. As you read his memoir, it should comfort you, as well. No doubt you will find yourself making mental notes along the way about things in Tim's story that never could happen to you (how many of us marry a billionaire's daughter?). But you'll find much more in common: things like the desire to prove yourself or to please others, or the gnawing idea that you're a failure despite all the evidence of your success.

I've been fortunate to meet with men and women all over the world who have come to a crossroads in life and made a decision to alter their path in radical ways. That's my journey—from a life focused mainly on success to one that centers on significance. In the twenty-plus years since I wrote *Half Time*, I've been amazed at the variety of stories I've heard over the years, but now come to expect the similarities of their threads.

And here's the most important thread: hope.

Whether you've always been wealthy and are realizing that wealth without purpose is meaningless, or whether, like Tim, you've fought for every dime and reached that same conclusion, you are never without hope. Whether you're at one of those inevitable low points in life, at a high point that feels empty, or on the brink of self-destruction, you can choose hope. You can step back, reassess, redirect, and choose the path of hope.

That path doesn't end one journey and begin another. As Tim shares, that path is part of the journey. The experience isn't something to be ashamed of, but something to embrace as you move forward to do great things in the second half of your life.

Tim's story is a compelling and at times dramatic account of an intense growth period in his life. He not only shares the journey, but also the lessons—practical ideas on how to shift your focus; how to bury the lies that hold you back; how to serve others and stop serving only yourself; how to embrace the pain of your past, work through it, and move forward into a life marked by joy.

For some of you, these are tips you'll want to implement immediately as a prescriptive medicine for the pain you're experiencing. For others, they will be preventive medicine—exercises that will strengthen your "spiritual muscle," as Tim calls it, and keep you healthy.

This is a book you will relate to on many levels, because you will see yourself throughout its pages. If you come at it with an open mind and a sincere heart, you will walk away with more than an interesting story about a man

who is surviving the fires of life. You'll also walk away
with valuable insights that will help you in your own
crucible moments. It will help you create your unique
story and, in doing so, it will allow you to share themes
and threads to help everyone around you. Like Tim, you
will help yourself and others. You will make a difference.

—Bob Buford
founder of Halftime, author,
and former chairman and CEO of Buford Television

# The Edge

Come to the Edge.
We can't. We are afraid.
Come to the Edge.
We can't. We will fall!
Come to the Edge.
And they came.
And he pushed them.
And they flew.

*Guillaume Apollinaire*

# Introduction

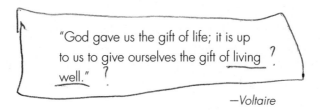

"God gave us the gift of life; it is up to us to give ourselves the gift of living well."

—*Voltaire*

WHEN I HAVE SHARED MY JOURNEY with others, I have discovered that my road, while unique, is filled with common potholes. My story is written through the eyes of a businessman, father, and husband, but it applies to you, whether you are single or married, a volunteer, homemaker, student, or fellow business leader. The pressure to balance expectations and reality can affect all of us, regardless of the positions we hold or our personal situations.

Many of us have experienced confusion, depression, and desperation. Many of us have felt trapped by life. Many of us have felt the need to appease others. Many of us have struggled to own our own values. Many of us have baggage from our childhood that makes it difficult to build and sustain healthy relationships as adults. Many of us struggle to give up control and trust that it will all just work out the way it is supposed to in the long run.

Some of you reading this may have lives that don't feel very stable. If the slightest thing shakes, everything around you will begin to topple like dominoes. For others, those symbolic tiles already lie in chaos at your feet. And still others of you are not really sure of your foundation. If any of this describes your reality, this book is for you.

I'm writing this book to tell you my story, but also, I hope, to help you with yours. Learn from my experiences. Use my mistakes. Embrace my lessons. Reframe your own story.

In its most simple form, mine is a story of redemption. It's the story of a man who, by having to face his pain in a dramatic way, went through a growth process, learned how to feel gratitude, reframe his own life, and have true joy.

In this book I share with you how I was sitting on the sidelines of life and truly living a life that no longer felt like my own. When darkness hit and I came to the Edge, I chose to "jump into the parade." People often wonder what that means. To me, it is a metaphor that means living in alignment with who you truly are.

I hope that my story will inspire you and, what's more, that you'll choose to join me on the journey—that you will jump into the parade of your own life.

BEFORE WE START, there are a few things you need to know.

One, I will be extremely vulnerable and transparent about some very dark places in my life. While I will not share all of the experiences, for fear of embarrassing or harming others, I will open the door far enough for you to experience my personal darkness. The truth is, I don't really believe in darkness anymore. It's simply the absence of light, and light is always there, even if you can't see it at that moment in time.

I've learned that being vulnerable and grateful increases my humility, which in turn, surprisingly, increases my joy. With humility, I see myself as I truly am. I don't think too highly of myself, nor too lowly. I don't sit passively like a doormat, but I acknowledge my weaknesses and am more transparent about my failures. I humbly acknowledge that I am a constant work in progress. I don't have the answers, but I have a deep commitment to continue to "do the work" as I continue on this journey. So, with humility, I'll openly take you back to a time not that long ago when I suffered in brokenness, because that low point for me was also my greatest teacher.

Two, I am a Christian and refer to God throughout this book. Please know that I also honor the fact that there are many who may not feel as strongly as I do about the Christian faith. Regardless of our religious or spiritual beliefs, we are all connected and can learn from each other's journeys, so I hope you'll read on and discover what you might learn from mine.

Three, reading this book may challenge you to live differently, so be prepared to make some hard choices about your values and how you live them out. This book is a collection of words, hopefully organized in a way that entertains and informs. Words create energy, which leads us to action. Action, in turn, creates experience, which shifts our perspective, causing our view of the world to grow and change. When you upgrade your language, you upgrade your life. I hope this book will inspire you to put into words the things you want to achieve. Be prepared to achieve them.

Chapter 1

# My Life Up or Down

"Before every great opportunity God
gave me a great trial."

—*Martin Luther*

TWO BUTTONS STARED BACK AT ME—silent, indifferent
to the pangs of my heart.

I could go up three floors to Prime, the Bentley Hotel's
rooftop restaurant overlooking New York City's East River
and Queensboro Bridge. I'd been there the night before,
walking outside to take in the majestic view of Manhattan and noting what waited on the other side of the short
balcony wall: a twenty-plus-story drop into nothingness,
a permanent solution to my temporary problems. That
nothingness beckoned this November night as I stood in
the hallway staring at the elevator buttons.

Up. The button could end my suffering. For years,
I'd been living in duality, acting one way on the outside,
feeling another way inside. I had thought that as long as I
stayed in motion, I'd be fine. But I no longer had the will to
run, and I wasn't sure if I had the will to stand and fight.

Breathing deep, I considered the other option: Down. In the lobby, a close friend and colleague was waiting for me. Somewhere beyond the pain and despair that tormented my soul, I knew this option offered hope. I had no idea what that meant or what it looked like, but something inside me assured me that hope was real. I just needed the courage to embrace it. Could I?

IF YOU HAD MET ME SEVERAL YEARS AGO, you would have thought my life was a happy rags-to-riches success story. By all appearances, you see, I had "made it." By my early thirties I was living the American Dream. I had a lovely wife and her supportive family, a beautiful son, a big house, two dogs, a group of close friends, and a thriving career. I had taken all that the world had thrown at me and come out on top. I had charged past my childhood, leaving behind my nomadic upbringing, a dysfunctional blue-collar family rife with drugs and alcohol, and all the educational naysayers who didn't believe I would ever amount to anything.

Just three decades in, I had achieved my every goal.

If my ambitions could be summed up in one word, the word would be "security"—the true thing I lacked growing up. I wanted the healthy, supportive, present family I'd never felt. I wanted the financial means, not because money was the ultimate goal, but simply to have the resources to protect my family from the life I'd once known. I didn't want my son to ever worry about whether we'd have enough money for groceries or be evicted from his childhood home.

For those very personal reasons, I was hell-bent on becoming a millionaire by the time I was thirty. And in fact, that's exactly what happened. By the time I set off for college at age seventeen, I was determined to graduate as quickly as possible so I could hit the ground running in my professional life. Early in my career, I was obsessive about learning every nuance about the company I worked for and the industry it played in, and was always the first one willing to volunteer for the most difficult tasks—simply for the opportunity and experience they might provide me. I did well and quickly climbed the proverbial corporate ladder, leaving my embarrassing and hardscrabble past behind.

On the personal side, I was equally focused on creating a relationship with a woman who would fulfill me and provide that safe harbor that I rarely felt as a child. This was driven largely in response to my greatest fear: being abandoned and unaccepted. Together, I reasoned, we would create our own family and provide a home for our children where they would always feel loved. A few years before I turned thirty, I fell in love with a woman, Libby, who challenged me both emotionally and intellectually. Her perspective on life stretched me in ways that I had never before experienced. With her, I always felt like life was an adventure to be discovered.

She was also the daughter of an ultra-wealthy businessman who had built his businesses and lived his life by practicing hard work, solid ethics, and determination. I soon found myself in the highest financial and social circles of Colorado. I was running a company and traveling the world. And a couple of years into our marriage, we had our son, the apple of my eye. Horatio Alger couldn't have written a better script for me. I was living my dream life.

But we all know about the deceptive quality of appearances, how perception is not always reality. Such was the

case with me. Behind the gated driveway, the member-
ships in exclusive clubs, the joys of parenthood, the flights
on the family's private jet, and a marriage of nine years,
my tightly knit life was coming apart at the seams. I was
smiling on the outside, but inside I was slowly dying.

I was one of the forty million Americans who suffered
from anxiety and depression, and in the decade following
my son's birth, the joys of being a father and the success at
work were often crowded out by dark thoughts, many that
had followed me since childhood. I learned later that life-
changing depression often rears its ugly head around the
age of forty-two—what some call a midlife crisis. Whatever it was called, it was hitting me hard.

Like many other affluent people, I often felt insecure
and guilty, and I had an overwhelming fear of failure. But
I didn't want to acknowledge any of that. I was depressed
on the inside, not from a chemical imbalance as some
people suffer, but by my continuous focus on not believing that I deserved to be loved or to be happy. I kept
pressing this depression inward, deeper and deeper, not
accepting it as true. I was caught up in believing I was
living the perfect life. It sure looked like it on the outside.
And the more I ran from the truth, the more comfortable
I was living a lie. I had created a false perception of my
"perfect life" and didn't want to face or deal with anything
that defied that perception.

In my hard-pressing pursuit to create my own personal utopia, I had never faced the issues that shaped me
as a person—the ones that had left me full of insecurity
and self-doubt, feeling unloved and, most importantly,
believing that I was unlovable and would never be fully
accepted. The ever-shifting temporal things I had built

my life upon—all of the achievements and acquisitions I thought would bring me joy and purpose—were not bringing the fulfillment I thought they would. In fact, I spent time focusing on the things I didn't have. I was stuck in a place of buried hurt that I couldn't seem to crawl out of. I could no longer keep the dark thoughts pushed down. They were rising to the surface, and I was being forced to face my pain.

I WAS IN MANHATTAN that November for another round of sales calls and meetings for Sign Language, a new large-format printing business I'd begun, and, frankly, I was doing what I did best: getting ready to make another pitch for my business. Taking action was my way of feeling secure and in control, and my way of ignoring all the warning signs. *Keep busy and keep working*, I kept rationalizing, *and everything will eventually sort itself out and be fine.*

For months, I'd actually thought I was winning the game. The sales at Sign Language were rocketing upward in a tough post-2008 economy, and our team of "A" players was getting stronger and stronger. Our strategy of doubling down and spending aggressively on infrastructure while our competitors were contracting had given us new market share faster than we'd anticipated. It was 2011 and we had finally turned the corner after starting the company from nothing three years before. I wasn't about to let the business fail—regardless of the market conditions. I was confident that if I just kept doing what I'd been doing, making calls and taking weekly business trips from coast to coast, everything would be all right . . . wouldn't it?

All the people around me at work had been saying the same thing: "You can handle this, Tim. You're okay."

My heart always knew the deeper truth: I was broken and no longer able to hide it from the world or myself. I wasn't winning, and my day of reckoning was at hand.

I had been engaged in a dangerous game of connecting my *works as a man* with my *worth as a man*. My habits of appeasement had taken me in the wrong direction, and I was honestly overwhelmed from trying to use my will to build a company faster than what the market was willing or able to provide. Working twelve to fourteen hours a day seemed like great protection, but it had walked me down a lethal trail that dead-ended in a box canyon. When my routine of nonstop action was parked for the day, I felt completely alone. The silence would come down hard around me, and the dark thoughts would come rushing in.

# Chapter 2

# Dark Thoughts

"Everyone you meet is fighting a battle
you know nothing about."

—Ian Maclaren

T HE NIGHT IN NEW YORK wasn't my first time battling the demons of despair. The first serious thought of ending my life came in July 2009, two years before the Bentley incident. At the time, I owned and ran a group of fifteen radio stations in Denver and the Rocky Mountains. The economic crisis that began in 2007 and ran through 2009 hit our industry hard, and one of the biggest players—CBS Radio—ended up quickly divesting its Denver stations for a much lower sale price than anyone ever would have expected. As a result, the value of all radio stations took a significant hit, and my stations, all bought when the market was high, were no exception. Advertising was one of the first line items to be cut from the marketing budget, and everyone in the industry was feeling the squeeze of reliable revenue streams and cash flow slipping away.

I made a tough decision in June 2009 to sell the Denver stations at a huge loss—as in millions of dollars in losses. Steve Cohen was the person I reported to at the Anschutz Corporation, the financial backer of the radio company, and someone for whom I came to have a deep respect as a trusted mentor over the twelve years we worked together. I came in to see him about an advertising campaign we were contemplating to boost Jack FM's listener ratings in Denver. We had gone through this drill before when we had ratings that were too soft to attract meaningful national advertising campaigns, and we had been unsuccessful in permanently moving our ratings. Steve challenged us. Did we really think we could generate enough permanent revenue growth to make up for all the losses we had incurred? Was anything really going to save us at this point? Inside I felt a profound sense of relief. I was grateful that Steve had asked us the one question that we had been too scared to answer for far too long.

My business partner and I left that meeting and took a hard look at our books, including the money we had borrowed and the compounding interest that we were racking up. The odds of us being able to stop hemorrhaging after servicing the debt payments for the stations were slim to none. We were completely upside down; the cost basis we bought the stations at compared to the current market valuation for the stations was far below what we had seen two years earlier, when we were in negotiations to sell all the stations for a small profit, and we were unclear on how to ride out the economic storm brewing in the United States and across the globe.

The business failure hit me hard personally. I was deeply ashamed, because the person I looked up to the most in life, my father-in-law, chairman of Anschutz

Corporation, had financed the radio business, and the losses affected one of his businesses that invested in growing companies. Even though the losses were mostly tied to the market crash, they happened under my leadership, and blaming their failure solely on market conditions did not allow me to own up to my responsibilities as CEO.

At age thirty-nine, it was my first large-scale failure, and I felt nothing but guilt and shame. I also felt lost at home—like I had failed myself and my family—because I'd failed in the one area where I always had attached my greatest sense of worth: my life as a business leader.

This was not how I ever intended to "show up" in the business community—I was supposed to always be successful; that had been the plan. Yet here I was, utterly broken, berating myself regularly and bereaved. My insecurities washed over me in waves throughout that year. My personal and professional lives had become an intricately intertwined rope, tied not to a stable post on the shore but to an anchor that appeared to be sinking in the middle of the ocean.

I spent many evenings living in the fast lane trying to keep up in the social circles we had become accustomed to. I was never fully present in that world, either. My mind was consumed with work, I was amped up on my relationship with Skoal (dipping tobacco), and I slept as little as possible.

Then, on a Saturday morning in July 2009, I walked out of the shower and realized that I was the only person at home. Libby and my son had left to run some errands, and our home was eerily quiet. Lost in my own dark thoughts, deeply depressed, and completely alone, I began thinking about the gun in the locked box at the top of the medicine cabinet. I took the gun from the cabinet, unlocked the trigger lock, and put it on the vanity. Then I sat on the floor of the bathroom for twenty minutes, thinking about what would happen if I put that pistol in my hand. Then I picked it up. Held it. Stared at it. *If I were gone*, I thought, *would everyone in my life be better off?*

Ironically, the pistol was originally for my protection. I had a concealed weapons permit for two reasons. One, owning radio stations in Denver put me in the crosshairs of some disturbed people who didn't always agree with the views expressed or the music played on those stations. Two, my office building was in downtown Denver near a bus terminal that attracted drug transactions. After some of those transactions occurred inside our office's underground parking garage and elevator, I bought a gun to protect my family, my coworkers, and myself.

In the training for the gun permit, they asked a question: Faced with peril, do you protect yourself first or your family first? The correct answer is yourself, because you can't protect your family if you don't first protect yourself. This time I wasn't protecting my family, or myself, from an intruder. I was the threat. Yet, the lesson still held true; I found the strength to protect myself from myself, and I set aside the pistol.

The thoughts of suicide, however, persisted. That morning in my bathroom, I had welcomed them in, offered them a comfortable chair and an ice-cold drink, allowed them to sleep over, and then suggested they move in and make themselves at home. Although I walked out of the bathroom thinking I was a stronger man, over the course of the next twenty-seven months, these dark thoughts began to completely control my life, and the stress and anxiety they created became unbearable. I went to the ER three times for severe chest pains and intense dizzy spells.

The thoughts told me I was a failure because I couldn't reconnect to the same vigor and passion that Libby and I had during our first eight years of marriage. They told me I was a failure for not recognizing the negative outside influences that had come into my relationship with my spouse. They told me I was a failure because the Denver radio stations had been decimated. They told me I was a failure and that I deserved nothing more than a one-way ticket back to my childhood, where every week of making ends meet was a flip of a coin.

Less than two weeks after the bathroom incident, my family took a ski vacation to Portillo, Chile. On the eight-hour flight into Santiago from Atlanta, anxiety hit me so hard that I thought I was going to die on the airplane. I began to suffocate, literally, from the stress and panic. Several nights later, I was sitting in our hotel room and felt myself start to crater. Panic hit me like a wave I had yet to experience. As I felt the walls close in around me, I knew this attack was bigger than I could handle on my own. I called my doctor in Colorado and he prescribed a small dosage of extended-release Xanax and a strong antidepressant. I didn't want to become dependent on anything outside of myself, but I took them because I felt like I was trapped and needed a way out, a new solution, and I knew that these prescription drugs, when used right, could be a life-saver.

A month after we returned from Portillo, I shared with Libby that I felt her parents deserved to know about my recent anxiety attacks, my experience two weeks earlier in my bathroom, and how I never felt able to live up to their expectations. I mustered up the courage to tell them all of this, plus how I felt that I was living a life I hadn't earned and wasn't worthy of having.

Knowing it had taken a lot of courage to be this vulnerable, my father-in-law looked at me and said, "Tim, I never asked you to live up to the expectations you have created in your head. I always wanted you to have access to different resources and people to build your business and your character. The more important piece has always been giving you the wisdom I've learned in life, many times from my own mistakes, to be a better man with the right set of values and perspective."

It hit me hard that night that not only were the expectations I had set for myself completely unachievable, but also it wasn't my father-in-law who had shackled them on me. It was me.

Still, despite my family's support and the medication I was taking, my pain intensified. By early 2010 I had lost self-confidence.

That September, I went dove hunting during an annual "ranch party" in northeastern Colorado that my wife and I hosted for nearly fifty friends and colleagues. There I was, walking through the morning fog with two of my closest friends, shotgun in hand and a vest full of shells. My friends decided to walk out of sight to hunt farther down a fence line so we would all be outside the range of a shotgun's pellets. Alone and suddenly afraid, I began, once again, to panic. The dark thoughts took over. This time, I fought back: I immediately broke down the shotgun and took out both 12-gauge shells.

I was forty-one years old. After months of this, I realized that my life deserved more than these thoughts that dominated my mind when I least expected it. I needed to be able to see clearly. I quit my prescription meds cold turkey in August 2011.

Once my head was clear, I didn't like what I saw.

I saw just how far apart my wife and I had grown. I had failed in radio, and now I felt like I was failing in my marriage. I knew it would take a commitment from both of us to make any meaningful changes. The dark thoughts fed on my plummeting self-esteem, my stress from working all the time to prove myself, and my growing resentment for living a life that was not my own. A maelstrom of emotions was churning inside me, ready to call the shots, and New York is where it would make its presence known.

Chapter 3

# A Cry for Help

"Don't measure the size of the mountain;
talk to the One who can move it."

—*Max Lucado*

WHEN WORK HAD ENDED EARLIER that day at the Bentley, I had retired to my room and, in keeping with my normal travel routine, I took a shower to shave at night so it took less time to get ready in the morning. As the warm water washed over my skin and swirled down the drain, my whole body began trembling. Something about hot water makes me feel fully alive and yet terribly vulnerable. Maybe it's because we're conceived and born inside the waters of life. Maybe it carries us back to those first, fragile moments of entering the world. Whatever the reason, on this night I stood there shaking so hard that I couldn't even shave my face.

I stepped out of the shower, looked in the mirror, and combed my hair, my hands still shaking and my chest hurting from what I recognized as an all-too-familiar anxiety attack. The memories took over—memories of all the times when the walls had closed in around me because I had failed, or thought I'd failed, as a man, as a husband, as a friend, as a business leader, as a father.

I sat down on a chair, wrapped in a towel and slumped forward, and I began to cry. Then, with the tears falling, I did what I always did when facing my biggest challenges and fears: I said the Lord's Prayer again and again. *Our Father in heaven, hallowed be your name . . .*

Repeating the words Jesus taught His disciples to pray was something that had often lessened my anxiety in the past. In 1992, when I went kayaking for the first time and found myself facing the wrong side of the raging Cache La Poudre River in northern Colorado, the Lord's Prayer came to me and calmed my nerves until I could pull the spray skirt and get free.

*Your kingdom come, your will be done, on earth as it is in heaven . . .*

When I was in my twenties and canoeing on Lake Yellowstone with my girlfriend and an unexpected and horrific storm blew in, I rhythmically pounded the paddle into the water as I prayed.

*Give us today our daily bread. And forgive us our debts, as we also have forgiven our debtors . . .*

When I became afraid while swimming in open waters in my first Half IRONMAN triathlon in Oceanside, California, I repeated the prayer until I was safely back on shore.

*And lead us not into temptation, but deliver us from the evil one.*

As I prayed on this night, there was no shore in sight, only the deep abyss. I felt a sense of both complete clarity, and deep anger.

Anger at myself, for failing, for not proving to the world that I was worthy, that I wasn't a failure. I'd been alive for more than four decades, and I had struggled through my personal wilderness for much of that time, looking for salvation. But I had been unable to find it anywhere. After all these years, I still felt as unworthy as I did as a child.

MY MOTHER WAS A SENIOR IN COLLEGE when she learned she was pregnant with me. One day, when I was just nine years old, my dad let me know that he had planned to break up with my mom until he found out she was pregnant. So instead, they got married.

But it didn't last long. By the time I was six my dad had resettled in Colorado, while my mom and I lived in Florida—first Orlando and, later, Pompano Beach. I felt ashamed because I had grown up as a member of the "working poor"—the only child of divorced, dysfunctional parents who, I believed, saw my birth as a "mistake."

I missed my dad a great deal, and longed for a male role model I could bond with. I remember once using five dollars in quarters I had earned from selling soda bottles to call my dad from a payphone at a local convenience store, just so we could talk for fifteen minutes.

Meanwhile, my mom was preoccupied with nurturing her drug and alcohol habits. Because she battled substance abuse problems throughout my childhood, we lived on and off with my grandmother, Nana. I credit Nana with most of the effort that went into raising me during the first decade of my life, but even so, there is not really a good emotional replacement for your own mother when you are a young boy. Children need affection, affirmation, and guidance, but I was given little of these.

When I needed boundaries, discipline, accountability, and self-restraint, I had to create them for myself. When things went wrong, I often had to find my own solutions. I don't associate childhood with carefree living or the joy of playing. While other kids were hanging out, I was working to help pay the bills when I was as young as ten.

My mother, unable to hold a full-time job because of her addictions and her lack of interest in developing a viable career, lived an unstable existence that left me in the care of the often not-so-loving public school system. My mom talked the officials at Tedder Elementary into admitting me to kindergarten after the birthday cutoff, which essentially placed me a year ahead of schedule. From then on I was always the youngest kid in my class. I also was typically the smallest, which became a problem when I was transferred to Sanders Park Elementary for second and third grade.

South Florida's schools had recently been integrated, and the desegregation system involved busing some students across districts. So in second grade, I rode a bus to a school where the classes always carried an edge of racial tension. Due to my size, I was an easy target for bullies, and I soon began living in fear of the bigger students who would contribute to some of my most memorable early scars—both emotional and physical.

One day in crafts class, I made a copper bracelet that I was very proud of and planned to give to my mother as a present. As I sat admiring the bracelet on my wrist after school that day, a much bigger kid in my class approached me and said he wanted it. Standing next to him were two friends of his—large, menacing boys. They were the same boys who more than once had come into the bathroom when smaller boys were in there, kicked open the stall, and pulled someone off the toilet seat. They lived to intimidate and humiliate anyone and everyone they could.

When the boys approached, I felt trapped, alone, scared, outgunned, outmanned, and outside my comfort zone. I didn't know what to do or what might happen next, but I got away from them as fast as I could. I went to the school office and called home. Surely my mom could and would rescue me.

She didn't see things the way I did. I asked and then pleaded with her to come get me, but she said she was busy and I had to be patient. She told me to wait for the late bus and tell a teacher if the kids didn't leave me alone. So I left the office and went outside to wait.

The three bullies lived near the school and didn't ride the bus, so my best hope was that they had gone on to other things. They hadn't. They were hanging around the area of the school where cars and buses dropped off and picked up kids, and it didn't take them long to spot me.

"I want that bracelet!" the biggest one said.

"You can't have it!" I told him.

He tore it off my wrist and towered over me, backed up by his two friends. I tried to get away, but the three of them beat the hell out of me. I rode home with my face bloodied and a split lip, the bracelet gone. I was embarrassed because the other kids saw me crying for the entire twenty-minute bus ride home. The bus pulled up in front of the apartment building where we lived with my grandmother, and I got out. My mother and a friend were sitting in folding chairs sunning themselves, stoned on pot and buzzed on white wine.

"Why couldn't you come get me?" I said through the tears. "Why couldn't you come get me?"

Totally self-absorbed and lost in her drugs and alcohol, she gave the impression that she couldn't have cared less. She told me I was fine, and I went inside, where my grandmother took off my shirt for me and cleaned my face.

At seven and a half years old, this marked the initial point of anger toward my mother and my earliest memory of my complete contempt for her narcissism.

EVEN AS A YOUNG BOY I was determined to prove myself worthy. No matter what my mother did and how much I felt neglected, I still wanted to please her, still desperately wanted her to love me. I had a daily routine of going around nearby apartment complexes and diving in Dumpsters for glass Tab and Pepsi bottles, recycling them for change so I could buy gifts for my mother. I saved enough money that I gave her a banjo necklace and a night on the Paddle Wheel Queen, a dinner cruise that sailed from a port in south Florida.

She loved the cruise, and she treasured the necklace for the rest of her life. When she died in March 2000, I found that banjo necklace in the top shelf of her jewelry box, which is where she kept the things she wore daily or simply adored.

During my childhood, her substance abuse only got worse; and it often led us into some less than ideal situations. For instance, once my mom was dating a rabbi from New York. No, this is not the start of a really lame joke. She literally was dating a rabbi from New York. Rabbi Dan was opening a synagogue in Florida. He had a wife and two boys back in New York, but for three years he "dated" my mother whenever he was in Florida. They spent a lot of time together without me, and I slowly became aware that she had converted to Judaism and that they weren't just casually dating.

For some reason, my mother brought me with her to New York to see the rabbi, so we drove all the way up the East Coast. While we were there, his affair with my mother apparently was exposed and, well, that didn't go over so well. I don't remember all the details—I was only eight years old at the time—but I do remember that I was sitting in the hotel room watching *Underdog* on television while Dan the rabbi had a discussion with my mother in the bathroom.

The muffled voices grew louder and louder until they broke my *Underdog*-induced trance and it dawned on me that they were shouting. I looked up and saw a body fly out of the bathroom and slam into the wall. My mother lay on the floor, her hair, face, and clothing disheveled, her face bruised and bloodied. I ran to her side, but Dan pushed me aside and told me to mind my own business.

"I'm coming back in half an hour," he told my mother. "If you're not here, I'm going to find you and kill you."

As a security deposit, he grabbed her purse with her money and walked out the door.

My mom decided to forfeit that deposit. Dan could have the money and everything else in the purse. She waited about five minutes, and then led me out of the room, down to the ground floor, and out a back door of the hotel.

I found a doorman and asked him to come to where my mother was hiding. She must have explained what was happening, because he retrieved the car keys from the valet and personally brought our car to us. We left everything behind and got into her pale yellow 1970 Volkswagen bug—"Puff," we called it—and took off for New Jersey. When we got there, she called my grandmother, who wired us some money, and then we drove nonstop back to south Florida.

True to his word, Dan came looking for my mom. He didn't find my mother, but he did have an encounter with my Uncle Donnie. My uncle got word one day that Dan was in town and that he was nosing around my elementary school in search of my mom. So Uncle Donnie came over and, well, he did unto the rabbi as the rabbi had done unto my mom. I didn't see the "eye for an eye"–type beating that Dan received, but my mother told me about it when I was much older.

As far as I know, Dan never came back. Then again, we didn't stick around Florida to see. In March 1979, a little over a year after we returned from New York, I was in the car with my mother when we exited Interstate 95 and came to a stop on Sample Road. Sitting at the stoplight, she looked at me and said, "Your dad wants us to move to Colorado. He's offered to let us move in with him. We're not getting remarried, but it might be nice for the three of us to be a family again. It's up to you. What do you think?"

I didn't realize it would be one of the most important decisions I'd ever make in my life, but I knew I wanted to move; I had tremendous clarity about that. I hated Florida, which should not be mistaken with a "dislike" for Florida. For starters, it was always hot; I know we didn't have air-conditioning in the car and I'm pretty sure we had none in the apartments we rented. I also associated Florida with always being on the move. We had never stayed in one apartment for long, so I never felt I had a stable home life. I wanted a change, a chance to build a new life, and I wanted to be closer to my dad. This move could give me both—plus the cooler Colorado weather. My heart said, "Go!" and that was all that mattered.

Of course, I was nine years old, so I also seized the opportunity for a little more. "If I can have a dog," I told my mom, "I'll move to Colorado."

A week later we were in the car driving across the country, and within days of arriving in Colorado I was introduced to my new puppy, Bucky, an eight-week-old black-and-white border collie.

## Chapter 4

# Sorrow May Last
for the Night

"From childhood's hour I have not been
As others were—I have not seen
As others saw—I could not bring
My passions from a common spring—
From the same source I have not taken
My sorrow—I could not awaken
My heart to joy at the same tone."

—*Edgar Allan Poe*

AS A TEENAGER, I struggled to fit in. My self-esteem was so low that I always felt I had to prove my self-worth. To prove that I was somebody.

My parents loved me. They were simply doing the best they could with the tools they had to work with at the time. My father had been abused and worked hard to break the cycle of abuse by loving me differently. My mother was abusing herself and tried to love me in the best way she knew how. I am thankful now for what love they showed me, but while I was growing up, I felt hurt, not gratitude, that they were emotionally absent much

**25**

of the time. I felt alone and insecure in the world. There was no safe harbor to which I could retreat.

This contributed to my perspective on life as I grew up. I saw the world as a cruel, unstable place. I adopted a victim's mentality and never felt deserving of any success, no matter how much I accomplished as a young man.

Before I'd even reached my teen years, I was absolutely determined that one day I would get out of Edgewater, our neighborhood outside of Denver, and make something of myself. And with each passing year, that determination only grew stronger. I'd get an education and then a good job. I'd make a lot of money and gain the independence that would free me of the limitations of youth. I wouldn't be bound by the decisions of adults who, in my opinion, didn't always have my best interest at heart. I wouldn't be held back by laws that limited my decisions because I hadn't yet lived eighteen years. I'd become the man I'd always wanted to be and show the world that I had, in fact, escaped, that I was somebody.

My single greatest goal of my youth was to escape the world I lived in—a world of bouncing checks at the grocery store, of no money for soccer cleats, of constantly moving, of having my birth certificate forged by my mom so I could work when I was only fourteen, of feeling like poverty was a prison into which I'd been unfairly sentenced. I believed that the way out of everything was simple: money.

In my twenties I quickly reached all my goals—and then some. I established my career in sales, experienced living and working abroad, made a very comfortable income, and felt the professional confidence that comes from consistently over-delivering on company expectations. I owned my own home and had no debt. I then met, fell in love with, and married Libby Anschutz, a smart,

talented, and beautiful woman I met in professional circles at work. Almost five years after first meeting, we
had our son. It was the stable, loving home life that I had
always dreamed of having for my family (and for myself).

With my marriage came an extended family that was
caring, industrious, and responsible. Libby was the daughter of one of the most affluent men in the United States
and one of the first billionaires in Colorado. This opened
all sorts of new doors for me, but most importantly, this
incredible extended family welcomed me with love and
support. The dichotomy of my past and present, however,
triggered many of my deeply rooted insecurities. I didn't
feel like I deserved it. Any of it. Not the money or status.
Not the stability, the acceptance, or the support. Not the
boards I served on, the suits I wore, the cars I drove, or
the home in which I lived. None of it.

I had everything I ever wanted and one more thing
I'd never bargained for: profound misery. All the success
and good fortune hadn't been able to erase my past; in
fact, in some ways it only intensified my pain.

I didn't belong in the world of the ultra-wealthy. Even
though I felt I had worked my way out of Edgewater—and
I sure didn't want to go back—I wasn't exactly at home
behind the gates in Denver. I had always been uncomfortable in social settings, and now I was mixing with some of
the wealthiest people in the country. They had the family
pedigree. They had the Ivy League education. Some had
earned their wealth and others were born into it, and
either way I felt they looked down on me. Even though
my résumé and professional accomplishments stood on
their own before I'd even locked eyes with Libby, I was
afraid of being viewed as the guy who "married into"
money rather than earning it.

Did I earn this access to capital, connections to CEOs at other companies, seats on various boards of directors, a membership in an exclusive country club, and—most importantly—the support of a patriarch who treated me like his own son? Regardless of how hard I worked or how much I achieved, I felt I hadn't earned any of the perks that came from marrying into this caring yet prestigious family.

The greatest value Libby's father brought to my life actually had little to do with money. He was the greatest mentor anyone could have had and I was fortunate enough to interact with him on an almost daily basis. All the security and stability and parental wisdom that had been absent when I growing up were provided to me now in my father-in-law. He opened doors—in the community and in the business world—and provided me with resources, but he didn't give me a free ride just because I had married into his family; instead, he gave me mountains of valuable advice about life and business. He gave me the tools of a solid foundation that no one else had provided to me while I was growing up.

To compound the feelings of insecurity and low self-worth that pressed upon me, in 2009, the Denver radio stations I was running, which were graciously backed by my father-in-law, failed spectacularly—I'm talking millions in losses. Because he had invested in the stations, and me, I felt as though I'd failed him, as well as Libby, who years earlier had gone above and beyond the call of duty and asked him to trust in me and back my radio station business plan. So, although I worked tirelessly over the course of seven years to try to build a fruitful and viable business, the market conditions, coupled with internal growth decisions and FCC regulations, led to a massive failure. What I'd worked for was crumbling before me.

And away from the office, my personal life was in crisis. I had a seven-year-old son I adored, but my marriage was starting to fall to pieces. Libby and I had spent the last few years unable to find common ground when it came to some core issues. Libby had just been named president of the Anschutz Foundation and was intently focused on supporting numerous education programs and positive nonprofit initiatives in Colorado. Our social circles began to change and there were new, competing influences on our time and attention that began to erode our intimacy and partnership. We were attending social events at a mind-blowing pace and not devoting enough time to preserving our relationship. Before the radio station went bust we had sold our comfortable home, one that finally felt like a real home and where I thought we would live forever, and had moved into a large, multimillion-dollar house that felt formal and cold. I walked through the door each night feeling like I was out of place in my own skin. Not that I did much to make it feel like a home. I threw myself into work, sleeping as little as possible and training thirty hours a week for IRONMAN competitions. My lack of focus on the relationship and Libby's involvement in other areas of her life and career led to more erosion in our marriage. It takes two to make a partnership work, and I will only speak to my side of the marriage and specific areas where I could have done better. I know I wasn't putting another's needs in front of my own or fixing my marriage and refocusing on the core of why Libby and I had become best friends in the first place.

My father-in-law saw that despite having so many good things in my life, I was deeply unhappy. Beginning in 2009, he repeatedly reached out to me to help, and he openly worried about my level of stress. He offered resources to assist me, including his own time, love, and commitment. He warned me of the dangers ahead if I didn't make some changes, and he encouraged me toward the changes I needed to make. He knew by that time that I felt trapped, partly because of his intuition about such things and partly because he was seeing clear warning signs. He made it clear I had options that I wasn't seeing. I heard his wisdom—but only with my head and never with my heart. I *understood* his words, but I wasn't ready to *feel* them. I wasn't ready to live them.

DESPITE THE DIFFICULTIES and pain from my upbringing, as a child, teenager, and even when I was in my twenties, I never considered ending my life. In fact, I couldn't even fathom such a plan. Not long after graduating from college in the autumn of 1991, I went on a hike with one of my oldest friends. I distinctly remember the spirit of optimism that filled the crisp Rocky Mountain air. We now had jobs that paid us enough money to eat something more than noodles, but mostly we had confidence in where we were going and we were embarking on a journey to have it all. And if we failed, so what? We came from nothing, right? We could just go back to eating Beanee Weenees and start over. As we talked about how incredible life was and how grateful we were to be alive, it seemed unimaginable that some people take things for granted or would think of throwing life away.

"I don't get it," I told my college friend. "Who in the world could ever consider suicide when times get tough?"

The answer? Me. Just two decades later.

Chapter 5

# The Decision

"He lifted me out of the pit of despair,
out of the mud and the mire. He set my
feet on solid ground and steadied me as
I walked along."

—*King David, Psalm 40:2 (NLT)*

WHEN I WAS THIRTY-TWO YEARS OLD, I was standing in Rose Medical Center at just past four in the morning holding a miracle in my arms. After more than fifteen hours of labor, my son had arrived well ahead of schedule, and all the emotions of a new father washed over me as I held my beautiful, healthy, newborn son.

Here was this tiny person who was just learning to breathe on his own, struggling to figure out the strange new world that awaited him, unaware of both the joys and challenges of life. And here I was, his father, blown away by his birth and acutely aware of the privilege and responsibility that came with being his dad.

He had done nothing in life but breathe and cry, nothing to earn the love or approval of me or anyone else, and yet the one thing he already had secured was my never-ending, unconditional love. I knew, as most parents do at this moment, that I'd give up everything, including my own life, for the sake of this child. For the first time I began thinking about my legacy. I wasn't just living for my life, but for my son's life and for his children and for their children.

And yet that night at the Bentley, I was totally self-absorbed. I wasn't even considering the magnitude of the lifetime damage I would do to my son, nine years old at the time, if I were to follow through with my thoughts to end my life. To do so would absolutely have altered the course of his life. It wasn't that I didn't care about that—I love no one more than my son—but I was in such a dark place that I simply couldn't see beyond myself at that moment in time. As I've since learned, people in the depths of depression typically lack the ability to truly think of others. It's a slippery slope of terror into a cavernous, dark, scary, and lonely place, where normal rules don't apply.

But something—or rather, Someone—kept me from making the selfish choice that night. Trembling and more afraid than I'd ever been in my life, I picked up the phone and called John, a friend and coworker who was staying in another room at the hotel. He was very calm and very direct, repeating his words a couple times: "Tim, come down to the lobby. I am going there now. Tim, come down to the lobby. I'll be there for you." He knew he wasn't going to get to my room in time to stop me, so he was trying to talk me into seeing that there was another option.

I made my way to the elevator, still unsure of what I would do. I stood frozen in time for what seemed like eternity before pushing the Down button. What gave me the strength and clarity in that moment? It was a very emotional experience, so it's hard to say for sure, but I believe I was guided by the unseen hand of God. I had been reciting the Lord's Prayer, and He was sustaining me. His grace broke through.

Even bolstered by His guidance, I still wavered about what to do. The elevator doors opened, and I got on but then hesitated. I stood in the elevator for eight to ten seconds—long enough for the doors to close and the elevator to just sit there, motionless, suspending me in my own purgatory.

Finally, I pushed the L button to head to the lobby. Somehow I knew going down was my only hope of ever going "up" again.

# Chapter 6

# A Friend in the Night

"The best way out is always through."

—*Robert Frost*

JOHN—JOHN C. GREENWOOD, CEO of Sign Language— was waiting in the lobby for me that night. As CEO, he oversaw the day-to-day operations, freeing me as chairman and founder to focus on sales, marketing, and business development.

John and I had talked some in the past about spiritual matters, and he was exactly the right person for what was happening to me on the darkest night of my life. We sat in that New York lobby for hours, and I went deeper with him than I imagined possible for two men to go. It was the unvarnished truth. We both confessed to how little we could control in life, regardless of how hard we tried or how much we thought we should be able to control.

He reminded me of a handful of simple things that will stay with me forever:

- I had more choices than I'd ever let myself see.

- I wasn't alone but was surrounded by a team of good people and friends.

- I needed to learn to celebrate my victories, instead of just dwelling on the losses.

- The last thing was more direct and heartfelt: I was wanted. "If you weren't around for the rest of us to be with, Tim, a lot of people would really miss you."

John arranged for me to get another room closer to the ground floor, and then he sat in that room the rest of the night while I slept. As I drifted off, I thought about three things:

1. The importance of being a strong father and involving myself differently in my son's life.

2. The fact that I'd been able to garner the focus and strength to pick up the phone and call John.

3. The first comment my father-in-law had made to me after I'd become engaged to his daughter in early 2000: "Life is simple if you always do the right things when no one is watching."

Then I thought about something else that Libby's mom had told me not long after we had gotten married: "The one thing that I tried to do as a mother was to give my children the right values to make wise decisions, because in life there are some choices that you make that you can never come back from."

Which button to push was one of those choices. By picking up the phone to call John and by pushing the Down button rather than the Up button, I'd made the right choice when no one was watching. Yet, I realized,

Someone was watching. I hadn't been alone in that room, just as I'd never really been alone throughout my life.

I'd spent a lot of time thinking about God, which is not the same thing as feeling the force of God's love in action. It's a hard concept to explain, but I believe God had been waiting for me to fully acknowledge my pain and to fully surrender—to fully turn my life over to Him and trust that everything would work out for the best with Him at the helm.

Like many of us, I was taught that religion and faith were all about having a strong belief system. If you believed in one thing strongly enough, other things were supposed to happen for you, predictably and on time. If you were certain of your spiritual convictions, you'd be both safe and saved. If you said you were all in with Christianity, the rest would take care of itself. That is religion lived in the head, not the heart, and I didn't know the difference. I believed in God, or tried to convince myself that I did, but I don't think I'd ever actually experienced God.

Even so, before I reached out to John, I had reached out to God. I don't know what I expected as I sat crying that night in the Bentley, contemplating my choices and reciting the Lord's Prayer, but by grace I had finally experienced God. I had stopped saying the Lord's Prayer and spoken my own words directly to God.

"I can't live like this anymore," I had said. "I can't do it. One way or another, this has to end. I need Your help, and I'll do anything if You'll take away this fear and pain."

I had wanted the torment to stop. All of it, right then.

In this dark moment a small, bright light had come in the form of a memory. It was a Sunday afternoon eight months earlier. I had been craving paternal wisdom. I was

constantly anxious and felt trapped inside the expectations I believed others had set for me at Sign Language.
I knew Phil could and would provide valuable perspective in a way that was always direct and rarely gentle. He
immediately found time for me that day at his home office.
I described some of what I was feeling, but I refrained from
telling him the entire story for fear of making him question my stability as a CEO. The voice inside my head was
running the tape of how I perceived his reaction would
be—*"Tim, you blew another opportunity to create a successful company. I trusted you and gave you capital, even after the
debacle with the Denver radio stations."*

However, when I met with him, the actual tape played
an entirely different track. He told me that CEOs often
make fatal decisions for their companies, and sometimes
in their lives as well, because they falsely believe they're
limited to only one choice. But the reality, he said, is that
they always have choices. He had been speaking directly
to me through this metaphor, but only now, in my crisis
in New York, did I really *understand* him.

The memory faded and I was back in New York. Ironically, since that conversation months earlier, my business
was now actually thriving on a very sustainable level.
Many of the sales seeds I had sown in 2009, 2010, and
throughout 2011 were beginning to bear fruit. Sign Language had gone from losing $400,000 a month in Decem-
ber 2010 to cash flow neutral in May 2011, and it had
remained there and turned a profit. The future seemed
bright.

But the turnaround had been exhausting. Success
and stamina in business can only take you so far if you
don't have the personal stamina to maintain the momentum. By that November in 2011, I'd been on a plane every

week that year and I was exhausted from constant business travel and ridiculously unhealthy hours. I felt like I couldn't let my foot off the gas pedal or we'd take a step backward in revenue the next quarter.

I wondered how one part of my life—the business part, where I was hitting singles, doubles, and sometimes home runs every week—could be so successful, while the other parts hurt so much. Why did I have three or four conflicted segments inside of me? Why couldn't I integrate all of them into a united and peaceful whole? For years, I'd believed that I could address each piece of my life in isolation, making a tweak in my business life or another at home or yet another in my spiritual life, and this would solve my problems.

Now I saw that I was overwhelmed and simply impatient for the situation to change. But I didn't yet have the clarity to understand that each of the pieces was interconnected and could only be dealt with as a whole. I'd never be a truly successful person until all were in alignment. Could I integrate the counsel I had received about leading a business with the right perspective about choices into all areas of my life? Could this free me from my trap? Did I really *have* choices?

In the silence that followed, something came to me, not as a thought, but as an emotion. For my entire life, I realized, I'd been fighting against what I thought I should be doing and thinking. I'd never taken the time or quit running long enough to uncover what was actually mine and what wasn't. I'd been living with what I imagined other people expected of me. I'd spent my life acting on the expectations I thought other people had for me without ever defining my own.

I wasn't living into alignment with my own values.

Then I understood for the first time that I could no longer manage my pain alone. It had gotten too big to carry. After decades of believing that I could control my life, my business, and my family, I knew I wasn't in control of anything, especially myself. This was much bigger than me. The pain and suffering had to stop, one way or another. Enough excuses, enough running, enough victimization.

A war raged within my mind. Did I really have choices? My pride told me that I could take care of the problems myself—by ending my life. But the opposite of pride is what I needed, and, thankfully, that's what I embraced that night in New York. It is what led me down, both literally and figuratively. Proverbs 3:34 says, "God resists the proud but gives grace to the humble." And that is what I did right then and there: I humbly acknowledged my need for Him.

The moment I did that, something shifted. The weight of the world left me, and for the first time in my life I felt as if I belonged. I was accepted. Approved of. No longer lost or trapped. If that's grace, I'll take more, please.

I had unconditional hope and could literally "feel it" running through my whole body. This new level of simply being—perhaps the word is "contentment"—settled into my heart.

One seemingly small step in the right direction opened up what had previously been sealed off from me: an opportunity to truly jump into the parade of life. My own parade. This was a chance to follow my heart and pursue opportunities that connected with my passions and values. I wasn't there yet, but I knew I no longer could watch from the sidelines or lead using values that weren't my own—or values that worked for only one segment of my life. I would now live differently, not by some blueprint I thought I *should* follow because someone somewhere—who even knows who—expected me to do so. My possessions, relationships, and successes (and my failures) would no longer define me.

I needed to stop appeasing others and to start building my own identity from the ground up. I needed to equip myself with the tools that would allow me to integrate all the pieces of my life into one whole and consistent person—at work, at home, and in the community. I needed to evict those dark thoughts from my head and stop believing their lies and half-truths. I needed to delete the word "depressed" from my vocabulary and, more importantly, from my reality. And I needed to adopt a new reality based on joy. I needed to move from victim to victor, and that's exactly what I planned to do.

SOMETIMES before you can move forward, you have to look back. You have to deal with that baggage you're carrying, because you can't take it all with you on the new journey. It's weighing you down and you're stuck until you lighten your load. Often we don't even know what that baggage is until we stop and examine it. Once we examine it, then we can reframe it. That was my next step.

Chapter 7

# Opening the Vault
# to My Past

> "Reflect upon your present blessings—of
> which every man has many—not on
> your past misfortunes, of which all men
> have some."
>
> —*Charles Dickens*

FLEW BACK TO DENVER after that night at the Bentley
determined to start my life over—not the easiest thing to
do at the age of forty-two. Where do you even begin with
that type of makeover? Could I fill a few holes with putty
and repaint a few walls? No, it wasn't that simple. Much
of my framework needed to be ripped out and rebuilt. I
had to get down to the foundation and reconstruct my
life. It was going to be a long process, a lifelong trajectory
of growth, a means of moving forward rather than being
stuck in the past.

Stephen McGhee would become a key person in this
process. Stephen is a life-leadership coach in Denver and

we had met two-and-a-half years earlier, when a mutual friend thought I might be interested in joining a team of men that Stephen was assembling to complete a nine-month program called The Aconcagua Man Project. The project was designed to push each participant to their physical, mental, emotional, and spiritual boundaries, ending with an expedition to summit Mount Aconcagua in Argentina, the highest mountain in the Americas, and the highest mountain outside Asia.

Stephen and I had met for two hours in 2009. At the end of the meeting, I told him I wasn't able to dedicate the time and mental commitment it would take to accomplish such a feat. We had not spoken since that meeting, yet for some odd reason, Stephen was the first person that came to my mind during my flight home from New York. He was the person I needed. He had made several comments during our first and only meeting that I had never heard before from another man. He was so clear and able to see the things hiding in my soul that I thought were well hidden. If anyone could figure out how to reach inside of me and help me rebuild my life, it was Stephen.

To my surprise, I still had his contact information in my phone, so I sent him a text message the minute the plane's wheels touched down in Denver. For whatever reason, my self-doubts about who I was as a man made me wonder if he would even remember me or even send a response. He did remember me, and he replied before I could get to my car in the parking garage. We met in person the very next day.

STEPHEN BECAME MY COACH, and as such, he quickly helped me formulate a life and leadership plan. The first thing I needed to do, he advised, was to start building "spiritual muscle." Mine had gone flabby from misuse or nonuse. It had taken me years to get into this state, he said, and it would take time and some heavy spiritual lifting to get out of it.

This wasn't exactly the message I wanted to hear. I was still pushing for a "quick fix" to my situation, but he wasn't open to that approach.

"I'm not going to throw a pill your way and have you think that you're better," Stephen said. "You'll have to unwind a lot of things that you've experienced, but never really confronted or processed or healed. If you're willing to do the work, I can help, but if you're looking for a halfway solution, then I suggest you find someone else."

I had other options, but I quickly realized that none of them would lift me up to the place where I could live my life differently, and with a clear purpose. I needed some tough love, and Stephen was there to offer just that—and only that. He wasn't there to tell me only the things I wanted to hear. He was going to challenge me and hold me accountable. And this would be a collaborative effort. I didn't have to go it alone.

I also realized that while a shortcut had at first seemed appealing, I was, in fact, willing to do the work. The easy way was building my house on shifting sand, and I'd done that long enough. I needed a sure foundation. I didn't care how hard it was or how long it would take. I decided it was worth it because I wanted to have my own integrity as a man and to define, once and for all, my own purpose and values.

"So where do I start?" I asked Stephen. "How do I build this spiritual muscle?"

"You'll need to start with focusing on your gratitude," he said. "I want you to fight for what you can be, not what you can't be, and that starts with being thankful for all the things you already have, all the things that are going well in life, and understanding what brings you joy."

My depression at the time was so severe that it coated my reality, and I couldn't see much of anything to be grateful for. My past and present were cold, dark, and gloomy, just like the Colorado winter, so that's the way I saw my future. I couldn't see the spring.

"Okay," I said a bit skeptically. "How do I do that? How do I focus on my gratitude?"

"Be grateful for everything."

This seemed like an unrealistic request, but I went along with it.

My first task was to buy a small clicker—the kind a venue employee uses when counting how many people attend a music concert. Each day I "clicked" my gratitude— tabulating all the things I was grateful for. To complete the assignment, I had to click it at least a hundred times a day—not an easy thing given the short, cold days and my still somewhat depressed state of mind.

With each click I expressed my gratitude out loud:

"I'm thankful for the dinner I just ate."

"I'm thankful for time I spent today with my son."

"I'm thankful for the heat in the vehicle that took me to work this morning."

"I'm thankful for the walk I just took."

Someone once told me, "It's the small things in life that really count." This was my first tool to relearn an important lesson that I hadn't fully appreciated or internalized the first time. Appreciating all the small but incredible things I had been taking for granted turned out to be the harbinger of springtime waiting in my soul to bud.

This not only made me far more appreciative of my life, but also a much better observer of everything and everyone around me. It also gave me the confidence and perspective I needed to observe the one thing I'd avoided the most: my past.

AS I STARTED BUILDING MY SPIRITUAL MUSCLE, I began looking really closely at where I'd come from and how it had shaped me—and how I'd allowed it to imprison me. I wanted to learn where the pain had started, accept it, and discover what it could teach me. What if I could reframe the most traumatic events of my childhood? If I stopped reacting to it or condemning it, what value might it have? For example, when I thought about the sadness and anger I felt at age seven when my mom neglected to rescue me from the bullies, I was able to reframe it to allow me to see that this experience provided me with motivation to make a meaningful difference in my own son's life.

When I reframed my past, I found myself humbled by the realities of it. The experiences of my past, I realized, were worse than some people's, but not nearly as traumatic as those of many, many others. I've met lots of people during my rebuilding, in fact, who had it far worse than I did as a child or an adult. I just never saw it that way until I started to experience gratitude for all that life had brought me.

When one wants to move forward, it may not seem like progress to look backwards—after all, that pain from my past and present is what led to my night of crisis. But there's a rearview mirror in the car for a reason: You don't look endlessly at it, but you do need to know what's behind you in order to direct your course on the road ahead. Looking into my past would help me learn from it and also free me from lies I'd believed.

IT ISN'T DIFFICULT to access the past. The small child we once were is still there, holding onto the memories and emotions that made us what we are today. All we have to do is open the door to our past and walk through it. So I did.

Chapter 8

# Carved by the Rocky Mountains

"Everything we feel is made of Time. All
the beauties of life are shaped by it."

—*Peter Shaffer*

COLORADO SHAPED ME. This was both good and bad,
or so it seemed during the process. Like the glaciers
that shaped the Rocky Mountains, the early experiences I
had in the Centennial State marked me in ways that were
painful at times. They shaped me in valuable ways, but
many of the best character-building lessons of my youth
were lost on me until much later in my life.

I was nine when we arrived in Colorado, and my mom
and I moved in with my father in a rental house in Arvada,
a northwestern suburb of Denver. A little more than a year
later we were all living in an apartment in Edgewater, a
largely working-class community in western Denver. For
three years, my divorced parents shared a living space,
but not a bedroom, to save money. I didn't have a bed to
sleep on, at least not a real one with a box spring, mattress, and frame. I slept on a mattress on the floor in the

same room as my father, until there was finally money for a full bed for me.

Soon, even as a child, I began earning my own way in the world so I could have some of the things I wanted but my parents could not afford. At age ten, I was helping my father install carpet. Whenever we left Edgewater in his blue 1976 Ford F-100 pickup and drove through wealthy Denver neighborhoods, I ducked down in the passenger seat, ashamed to be seen in his vehicle. I didn't belong in those neighborhoods or around those people. They were better than I was because they had more money.

By the sixth grade I had a *Denver Post* paper route, and by the seventh grade I had started my own business selling gum and candy at my school. I'd buy chewing gum for nineteen cents a pack and sell it to my classmates for half a dollar. The business lasted several weeks until the principal made me shut down, but by then I had managed to save enough to purchase an Atari system for $138.

During my childhood, my mom told me two things that have stuck with me for life. First, she said, the world owes you nothing. That's a good perspective in the society we live in, where so many have a sense of entitlement. Second, and more important, she told me that the one thing in life you can't afford to lose is your good name. Both of those pieces of advice sat firmly in the back of my mind as I began making my way in the world.

When I was sixteen, my mother and I got into a bit of a standoff. By this point, we were not living with my dad anymore. At first we were living with a man who promised to marry my mom but who cheated on her all the time, but that ended shortly after my mom had her own rock-bottom moment. After nearly killing us while driving drunk and high one night in 1985, she finally recognized she needed to change. So we moved out of the house we were sharing with this man, moved into an apartment in Lakewood about four miles south of Edgewater, and my mom began attending Alcoholics Anonymous. Soon she was a recovering alcoholic who had become a born-again Christian and who now wanted to have more influence over my life.

But after so many years of seeing her as an absentee parent, I was angry and had zero interest in giving her respect and playing by her new, strict rules. I had severe anger issues about her expecting me to now forgive her, and I didn't like her new boyfriend, who was her sponsor at AA; they were dating even though the organization frowns upon a romantic relationship between members and their sponsors.

As it turned out, that boyfriend would become her husband the following year. As I've learned to reframe my mother's life and the choices she made, I realize that he was an incredible man who stuck by her through breast cancer until she died in March 2000.

At the time, however, I rebelled against my mother and her new boyfriend, and I made the decision to move in with my father. The timing was right because the week before, my father had suffered an on-the-job accident. It left him disabled and limited his ability to work. We didn't have the money for him to see a doctor or get pain medicine, so he literally spent most of the next three months lying, and living, on the floor.

While still in school I got a job at Azar's Big Boy waiting tables, so I was now taking care of him physically and paying the majority of our bills, working the dinner to late-evening shift. When we couldn't make ends meet, I'd go to the manager and ask for more hours than a sixteen-year-old was supposed to work. Azar's bent the rules and let me have a few more hours so we could get by. I would clock out as scheduled, but Matt and Carla, the managers on the evening shifts, would let me stay on duty and work for tips.

Working in the food service industry taught me a great deal about business and customer service, but it didn't help me get more sleep or provide more time to study. Algebra II was my first class each morning—not a good time for me to take the many quizzes and exams the teacher gave. After working at Azar's until after midnight, I was exhausted when I stumbled into the classroom each morning and often fell asleep at my desk. The other kids teased me, and the teachers wondered why I didn't have better focus. I was too embarrassed to tell anyone I was working the late shift to earn enough money for Dad and me to live on.

Because I was working close to forty hours a week my junior year, I missed out on homecoming, the prom, and many other social activities. I kept working so I could pay our rent, utilities, and other living expenses. Dad tried to earn money through telemarketing, but that created other problems—he ran up a $400 telephone bill while lying flat on his back. However, I appreciated my father's efforts to find a new source of income for us, and I didn't mind putting in the additional hours.

I occasionally would see my mother at Azar's with her AA group, where they would drink coffee and smoke cigarettes. I made the mistake of complaining about how tough things were, and she responded with, "Your choices and your consequences." In retrospect, she was right, and what I was doing to support my father was also right. It is funny how hindsight, and reframing life, is always 20/20.

Once, when money was very tight, we qualified for food stamps. When I went to the store to use them, my self-esteem was crushed. I felt deeply ashamed using the stamps to buy cheap, generic, frozen turkey pot pies. At the checkout line, I threw the stamps down on the counter and looked the other way, unable to meet the clerk's gaze. And when I got home that afternoon, I tossed the remaining stamps in the trash for good.

"I'd rather starve," I told myself, and then my father, "than go through that again."

To cover our bills, I once again talked my boss into bending the rules and giving me a few more hours. We got along on a diet of potatoes and those generic frozen pot pies. We stayed afloat, but my studies inevitably suffered. I learned the value of hard work and ingenuity, but I struggled to value myself. I felt defined by my circumstances— limited by my choices, always feeling broke, the sense that there was always "money drama" in our home.

I was ashamed to accept handouts from the government, but I began to fear letting down the people I cared about or who had some influence over my life. I felt I had to please or appease everyone around me just to survive— a bad habit that would only get worse as I got older. And I felt the pressure to be the provider for my dad.

But I was also angry at my dad, and my mom, because I didn't believe they wanted me. Rather than being thankful that they chose to have me, I saw myself as a "mistake." I was ashamed of who I was, and I felt I had no real value as a person. But I kept these feelings hidden, pushing them down into an emotional abyss. Letting these feelings out would only cause trouble. I couldn't cause waves. I had to "man up" the best I could, keep my job, and take care of my dad. It made no sense to me at the time to deal with the root causes of the things that were provoking my feelings.

For instance, when my mother started going to Alcoholics Anonymous, she insisted I attend meetings with her. I believe she had come to terms with how absent and difficult she had been in my life, and she wanted me to understand the mistakes she (and others in our family) had made with alcohol so that I'd be equipped to make better choices. But I had deep disdain for being forced to be there. I was trying to gain control over my life, but so many others were dictating how it should be. Rather than addressing my issues related to her addictions, or being happy and supportive of her new life choice, I shoved everything I felt further inside. If it went down far enough, I kept thinking, it would just stay there for good.

In my mind, I was a victim—of my mom's drinking, of my dad's bad back, of not having enough resources, and basically everything wrong that had ever happened in my life, including things I'd brought on myself. No wonder I was driven to leave my childhood experiences behind when I graduated from high school. No wonder I thought that money was the answer to all of life's problems. No wonder I was so determined to pursue financial success and security above all else. I didn't yet understand that scarred memories and emotions don't care about dollars and cents, or about time and space. I didn't yet know that the little kid who'd gone through all this would still live inside of me, calling the shots.

FOR YEARS, I literally denied that I'd ever been a child, and I certainly didn't want to repeat my growing-up years.

I recall being with friends once in my late twenties and listening to them talk about how great their lives were as kids. My victim's retort came like a knee-jerk reaction: "I wouldn't go back to being a child for all the money in the world."

I still feel that way, but now I realize that without all my childhood experiences, I wouldn't be the man I am today. When I was able to reframe my life I realized that everything I've gone through has shaped me and equipped me for the opportunities God has planned for me. We're never free from our most troubling emotions until we finally stop and confront them, whether we're nineteen or ninety-five. Emotions and feelings are not rational. We can't argue with them. But we can learn the origins of our emotions and why certain things make us feel certain ways. Then we can choose how to use those feelings and emotions.

As I began to reconstruct my life, I began to learn that I had a choice about those emotions: I could acknowledge them but choose to not let them control me.

AT THE BEGINNING OF MY SENIOR YEAR, I briefly moved back in with my mother after my father's back healed and he decided to move back to Florida to secure better carpet installation opportunities. My mother and I lived together for two months before her company, AT&T, downsized their Denver operation and relocated her to Atlanta.

On my seventeenth birthday, my mother departed for her new home in Georgia. She gave me the option to finish my senior year of high school in Atlanta, but I was not receptive to starting over again in another school. Several of my friends' parents—good, middle-class, hardworking people—stepped up and said they'd lend a hand with my boarding until I graduated from high school. Fortunately one of those people was my best friend's mother. I moved in with Mike, his mother, and his younger sister in the middle of the first semester of my senior year.

They lived in a tri-level duplex with three bedrooms, and I was now the fourth person. So that I could have my own room, Mike's mother hung a sheet over the door of the downstairs family room and called it my new bedroom. She also was kind enough to give me more than just food and a bed—she nurtured me as a human being by allowing me into her family, treating me like one of her own—giving me respect, dignity, and love.

She worked the graveyard shift at CoorsTek in a porcelain factory, earning very little money, yet she opened her home to me. She made certain that I had a family to "come home to" at night. You never forget these sacrifices, or the feelings around them, or the people who have made your life better. I was thankful at the time, but it wasn't until my late twenties that I truly realized the magnitude of their sacrifice.

At seventeen, I graduated from high school and enrolled at Colorado State University in Fort Collins. My paternal grandparents gave me money for my tuition and dorm expenses for my freshman year, and I volunteered for the ROTC with hopes of earning an Air Force scholarship and becoming a pilot. At the end of my first semester, the colonel reviewed my scores from the Air Force Officer Qualifying Test. The results would help determine my future in the Air Force once I became a commissioned officer. My score qualified me for the copilot or navigator path, but he told me all the slots for white males had already been filled. The officer told me that my most likely path would be as a nuclear missile officer in a silo somewhere or in an information technology role, but all the scholarship slots for white males for those positions also had been filled. I didn't have the funds to continue college without a scholarship.

I hadn't been particularly responsible with the $3,000 my grandparents had given me to pay for my first year of college. I've always loved cars because they've always represented freedom, so what did I spend my grandparents' money on? Cars. And after buying a used 1965 Ford Falcon *and* a 1970 Ford Bronco, I had nothing left for my second-semester dorm fees. So I dropped out of ROTC, started working at restaurants, and set up a delayed-payment plan for the housing costs at my fraternity during my sophomore, junior, and senior years.

For the spring semester of my freshman year, I moved into a house with two seniors who needed another roommate. I worked a few odd jobs to pay my share of the rent, but I had no furniture, so I slept on an old couch in the living room. They grew so tired of seeing me stretched out in the living room that they gave up the community couch and moved it into my bedroom.

I was also pledging Sigma Nu at the time, so I spent a good bit of the semester drinking beer when I should have been studying. Some of my best friends today are fraternity brothers, but I never enjoyed the full experience in college because I missed many of the social events so I could work, and my self-esteem suffered because I felt I wasn't paying my way. Most of my meals came at the Sigma Nu house or by working during lunch at one of the sorority houses, where being fed was the payment for serving and cleaning up after the ladies in the house finished their meals.

After my freshman year, however, I took school and work far more seriously. I was out of money, and it was clear that my fortunes in life were not going to be found without a college degree.

I had a victim mind-set about my Air Force ROTC plans being foiled, but I shifted my anger and energy to focus on graduating early. I took eighteen to twenty-four credit hours per semester, graduating from CSU in three and a half years with a degree in political science. I was extremely restless to put school behind me; I was ready to be a fully grown-up adult, out in the world, building a career and making money. In time, I came back to CSU and got involved with raising scholarships for students from rural communities and in other alumni activities. I love, support, and remain active with CSU now, but back then, my years in college seemed like a huge waste of time, a necessary chore for a piece of paper that would help me get a job and open up doors that would put money in my pocket and give me the security I always craved. I was tired of waiting for my adult life to begin. I was ready to move forward and never look back—I even purposely refused to look in the rearview mirror as I left campus after my last final exam.

As a working adult, I could finally get away from my upbringing and bury my vulnerabilities once and for all. I could finally be somebody. I could have my own place— or, at least to start, a bed in my own room. I could buy a new car instead of used ones and have extra cash at the end of the month after all the bills were paid. I was determined to live debt free and never owe a nickel to anyone. Most importantly, I could truly leave the past behind. I could finally get started on life—on my terms. I would be the one calling the shots. I would live on "my time."

So as I drove away from CSU that cold December evening after finals, I told myself repeatedly that now my life was really beginning.

Chapter 9

# Taking Off the Victim Pants

"Do you want to know who you are?
Don't ask. Act! Action will delineate and
define you."

—*Thomas Jefferson*

My FIRST "CAREER" JOB was in the Denver corporate
office at Pace Warehouses, which later would be
acquired by Sam's Club. I was hired at $20,000 a year for
an entry-level purchasing position. I bought small elec-
tronics and computers for each store, and I struggled to
find any challenge in the role. I've always had an entrepreneurial spirit, so I got bored quickly with a nine-to-five
desk job.

One night while watching the movie *Point Break*, I
was rattled by the words of Patrick Swayze's character.
He was talking to his partners about not wanting to be a
soulless person driving to work each day in a metal coffin,
trapped in a job and/or life he didn't love. I could relate
to his angst and the words stayed with me.

After eighteen months I quit Pace and moved into
the high-tech field at American Power Conversion (APC),

where I could better use my skill set and make a difference. I was working for the company that helped create the market for uninterruptable power supplies and surge protectors targeted for users of personal computers, network servers, and data communications equipment. For $24,000 a year plus a small quarterly sales bonus, I helped ramp up APC's warehouse sales and both reseller and wholesale distribution channels.

In May 1994, about a year and a half into this job, I was in Rhode Island for the annual all-company sales meeting. While there, the global vice president of sales asked me if I'd be interested in opening up American Power Conversion's first sales office in Australasia, covering Australia, New Zealand, Papua New Guinea, Fiji, and Tahiti. Five weeks later I arrived in Sydney with four suitcases, my passport and visa, no credit history, no cell phone, and no real clue where I was going to live. But I was on an adventure and felt like somebody. I was representing my company in a larger, international market. It was especially exciting because I was just twenty-four years old. I found Australia to be an easy place to meet people, conduct business, and begin to plant semipermanent roots.

I could have lived there much longer, but my life abroad came to an abrupt end almost a year later when I received a call late one night from my mother. I was at the Perth Airport, just getting ready to board a red-eye back to Sydney, when she let me know that she had just been diagnosed with breast cancer again and it was spreading to different parts of her body. I couldn't sleep the entire flight to Sydney and kept thinking of the best way I could support her. On the phone my mother had encouraged me to remain abroad, but by the time my flight landed, I'd made a decision to come back to the United States so I could be there for her.

My former sales position with APC in Colorado had been filled, so I worked for the company in Kansas City and then in Chicago with another company called Xircom, before returning to Denver. The next couple of years I bounced around, quitting Xircom shortly after returning to Colorado to begin working for a startup division of Canada-based Newbridge Networks, a telecommunications equipment maker. But my tenure there finished suddenly when it laid off its U.S. sales force for the division of the company I represented. In January 1998, I took a position as major account manager with Cisco Systems. With each job change my salary had been increasing, and it jumped significantly as my sales numbers took off at Cisco because I was making commissions on sales of equipment that sometimes cost more than $50,000 for a single piece of hardware.

Joining Cisco turned out to be among the most impactful decisions up to that point in my life. I now was with the most prestigious name in the high-tech industry for networking equipment. I would always get my calls returned because it was Cisco Systems. It was also the first time I had a boss who really challenged me to think differently—both in what I did professionally and with my personal decisions.

For example, I went against his advice and bought a new Corvette convertible with the money I earned one month. He was very vocal on conspicuous consumption and how spending my money on a car this fancy made me look bad personally, and to my customers if they saw it, and was also a waste of how that money could be used in terms of investing in a future family. He was completely right.

My boss was a no-nonsense, tough-love guy with a degree from The Citadel and no tolerance for my victim mind-set. He pushed me, taught me, stretched me, and mentored me, in life and in business. As a result, I was seeing the fruits of success.

I was in my late twenties, making more than $600,000 a year, and working for a great boss at a solid and well-respected company. Ten years earlier I'd been in high school living in a curtained-off section of a friend's living room, and now I was able to buy my first house. I didn't like taking on debt, but I did take on some in order to make this purchase. However, I paid off the mortgage in just fourteen months. My biggest motivator in paying it down so quickly was fear. After losing my job almost overnight with Newbridge Networks, I'd felt financially vulnerable, much like I had in my teen years when the burden was on me to pay the bills for my dad and me. By paying off my house, I felt more powerful and in control. In fact, I went to another extreme and began to run credit balances for most of my recurring monthly bills. My friends thought I was insane to tie up that type of cash, but I thought it was imperative to have a financial cushion. I refused to feel the stress and shame I felt when I was growing up. I needed to feel in charge.

My job with Cisco also connected me to the rapidly growing Denver-based telephone company, Qwest Communications, which is where I met my future wife. Libby was one of my clients, working at Qwest in product development. We worked together for most of 1998 until she relocated for six months with Qwest in San Jose,

California. We went on our first date not long after she moved back to Denver in May 1999, seventeen months after we first became friends.

We dated for six months, and then I asked Libby's father for permission to marry her. We were engaged for almost a year, and then in August 2000, Libby and I were married in an incredible ceremony at Trinity United Methodist Church, one of the oldest and most beautiful churches in downtown Denver. In addition to the pastor who married us, Bob Beltz—the pastor that Libby had grown up with—conducted part of the ceremony. At the time I had no idea that this childhood pastor of hers would later become a critical person in my recovery from depression. Twelve years after the wedding, on a snowy afternoon in January 2012, two months after my New York turning point, Bob sat down with me for lunch at a restaurant in downtown Littleton, Colorado, and shared with me a number of stories related to how people had reframed their perspective of life possibilities, beat depression, and went on to live more joy-filled lives. This conversation provided me with a huge spark of hope and reminded me how God works miracles through other people.

When Libby and I first married, however, the idea that I would ever need such advice would have seemed crazy to me. I was thirty. I had a thriving career, substantial assets to my name, and no debt. All of the emotional issues I needed to deal with were, for the time being, sufficiently glossed over by my worldly success. The future seemed bright. On the surface, there seemed to be no reason why I *should* have any lingering doubts and fears about fitting in around successful people. But no matter how much money I made, I didn't feel financially safe (though I thought I *should* feel that way). Instead, I still felt trapped. I hadn't yet discovered that "shoulding" doesn't work (I'll explain this concept in chapter 16). I began trying to live up to the expectations I thought my father-in-law (and others) had for me. I thought I needed to portray myself in certain ways and live differently because I was now part of a prestigious family. Any little setback—or perceived setback—simply exposed my fragile emotional nature. I still felt like I had to please everyone around me. On the outside I looked like a man with a future, but inside I was still letting myself be a victim of my past. Libby's father recognized it before I did. In fact, the most pointed criticism my father-in-law ever made of me was that I spent too much time wearing my "victim pants" whenever something went wrong.

"I know you want to be an entrepreneur and a leader," he once said. "You need to start recognizing that you're going to have twenty-nine difficult days and then one incredible day, where you really move the ball down the field. If you're willing to grow a Teflon skin and let things roll off of you and keep charging forward, if you're willing to trust that you know you're moving in the right direction, you'll eventually be victorious. Building something meaningful is hard work, and if it were easy, everyone would be doing it. I strongly suggest you make a lifelong decision to lose your victim pants. They will never serve you positively."

More than anything, for my own freedom and in part to please him, I wanted to take those defining pants off for good, but that's much easier said than done. As children, we develop elaborate coping mechanisms that once served us well because they helped us survive and live with our pain. We naturally revert to them, but are they

really what's best for us now? Do we want them control-
ling our adult lives, or do we want to forge new patterns
of thought and behavior?

As children, we are, in many respects, helpless. We are
at the mercy of conditions we have no control over. We
don't choose our parents or our childhood environments.
However, as we grow older, we get to decide how these
childhood coping skills transfer into an adult life. For
me, I had coping skills disguised as bad habits. One such
skill/habit was that of always staying busy and moving
from job to job. I recall being with my mother during one
of her Alcoholics Anonymous meetings, and the speaker
was talking about how people will move to a new city to
flee from the current problems they've created for themselves. What they discover is that they re-create those
same problems; their patterns of being a victim and/or
using the same methods of living their lives and making
decisions continue to yield the same outcome. It's like that
one definition of insanity: doing the same thing over and
over again but expecting different results. Reacting from
a victim mentality is no different.

As a small boy, I learned to attach an outcome to a feeling. If I felt alone or fearful or abandoned—as I did on that
day I was beaten up at school or the day I watched Rabbi
Dan knock my beat-up mother to the floor—I wasn't just
upset. I was literally afraid I might not survive—an appropriate feeling for a small child under physical attack. Such
a reaction is wired into us for our protection; it unleashes
the fight-or-flight impulse that may in fact save our lives.
But for me, an unhealthy pattern developed from this
and followed me into adulthood. This entrenched coping
mechanism of continually fighting for my survival stayed
with me throughout my thirties, and was finally brought

to a critical head that night in the Bentley Hotel, when the old feelings and issues came flooding back into me and would not easily be abated. I wasn't under physical attack, but I was trapped in my own mental and emotional anguish. I was afraid to die, but I also was afraid to live. I had programmed my brain to see only one way out of such pain: total escape. It wanted fight or flight, and I didn't have much fight left in me.

When I returned to Denver after that episode and finally committed myself to real change and to building spiritual muscle, I learned a new tool: how to separate a feeling from an outcome. It took self-awareness and discipline to stop my sense of panic and spiraling down-ward just long enough to realize that I didn't have to be beholden to these feelings and memories. I had other choices, if only I'd let myself react in a way that allowed me to explore more than one outcome. I could choose to slide further and further out of control—or I could choose to be victorious in the moment by reframing the situation.

Each of us defines our sense of victimization in the world—or our sense of victory. A very slight turn of feeling and perception can shift the entire way we see ourselves operating in the world. That reframed perspective is the difference between being a passive victim or an active participant in life.

ONE UNEXPECTED CONSEQUENCE of using that clicker a hundred times a day and becoming more grateful for everything was that it helped me reframe my life and realize my background was actually the reason I survived that night in New York City. I had fallen back on the toughness and strength I'd learned in Edgewater as a child to fight back and survive.

My commitment to building the spiritual muscle ultimately boiled down to one thing: I wasn't going to negatively impact my son's life. I was forty-two, and my son had just turned nine. We were about to enter a critical time in our shared journey. That single thought became the turning point in my life. I had the power to make other choices and to change my feelings from being a victim to being a victor—not just for my sake, but for my son's.

Once you choose not to be a victim, once you decide to look honestly at what's shaped your emotional reality, you're not going to be instantly transformed into a new person. You still feel pain—lots of it—but as you heal and grow, you feel the pain of old habits or bad patterns of appeasement literally leaving your body.

The key thing you learn during a transformation is that people simply don't know the life they're not yet living. You haven't yet imagined that other life because it isn't entirely your own. The unimagined life opens up when you stop resisting.

You then have to step into the unknown.

Chapter 10

# Playing the Right Tune

"Develop interest in life as you see it;
in people, things, literature, music—the
world is so rich, simply throbbing with
rich treasures, beautiful souls, and
interesting people. Forget yourself."

—*Henry Miller*

ENJOYED WORKING in the high-tech industry, and I had learned a great deal during my years there about both life and business. But I soon grew tired and was ready to embrace new challenges. Libby and I had been married for a couple of years, and our firstborn was a few months away from arriving on the scene. I was in my thirties, mid-career, and itching to set out on my own. The entrepreneurial bug had landed and was working its magic. My father-in-law, sensing the dissatisfaction building within me, suggested I find something I was genuinely passionate about and could commit to. We went for an hour-long bike ride on a sunny August afternoon and he offered to help finance my first real venture as an entrepreneur. I began designing a company around my greatest passion as a young man: music.

In and around all of the challenges of my childhood and adolescence, music soothed, comforted, and nurtured me like nothing else. Music somehow instantly connected me to my heart and made up for life's disappointments. It set me free and generated euphoric feelings that words could not describe. At night when I was anxious and couldn't sleep, I'd tune in to the small radio by my mattress and listen to songs from all over the dial. Pop and rock put me in touch with a deep feeling that carried me away from fear and pain, from anger and resentment, and from the sense of failure. For the few moments while one of my favorite songs was playing, shame and fear fled. I was good enough for anyone or anything, and many times the lyrics of the songs helped me to imagine what life could someday be like.

As I grew older, I listened to U2, The Smiths, Alison Krauss and Union Station, Robert Earl Keen, The Band, Derek and the Dominos, Paul McCartney, and countless other artists, some known worldwide and others quite obscure. Over the years, I put together what I would argue is one of the largest music collections in Colorado.

Music also formed a shared bond between my mother and me. No matter our conflicts, there was one thing we both loved: music. As a child, when I'd sit beside her in the front seat of the car with the radio blasting, the two of us would sing along with Elton John or the Bee Gees, neither of us thinking about the things that came between us or of our individual pain.

So as I considered where my passion intersected with my entrepreneurial path, I thought about my love for music, the mystery and excitement of radio, and those early days of singing with my mother as we rode together in the car.

By this time in my life, I'd grown to love and respect my mother because of the woman she eventually became: a woman who learned to defy her demons and jump into her own parade. As I shared earlier, my mother entered AA and drastically turned her life around. She died of breast cancer when I was thirty, and by then she had remarried her AA sponsor and moved back to the South. During the last eight years of her life, she was intent on helping other breast cancer patients and developed friends all over the world. She became very close to a woman in China whose husband was high up in the Communist Party. Despite China's censorship rules, they could email back and forth because of her husband's political position.

At her funeral, a hundred or so women of all races, some bald and in full chemo, showed up to share powerful words about my mother and what she'd done for them when they were going through treatment. I looked at all the people who were there and realized that once she'd become clean and sober and reframed her life, she had spread a lot of beauty and grace into this world.

I believe my mom was able to create pure goodness in this world because she was an alcoholic and a substance abuser. She had gone through the fire and the crucible. She emerged selfless in her focus, and her own demons gave her a unique perspective on what it meant to fight for an unencumbered life.

I reached into her open casket and put my hand on her hand, looked lovingly at her face, and quietly said goodbye. She was gone and a chapter of my life had ended.

I buried my mother and with her one ragged piece of my own emotional life.

The idea of pursuing a career centered on music grew stronger because it connected me to my mother and helped keep alive my most prized memories of my life with her. It just felt right. This period in 2001 when I started exploring music as a career choice actually got me very close to jumping into the parade, but it would be another ten years until that night in New York before I was truly all in.

In 2001, I was following my heart and pursing personal and business opportunities that connected my passion and values. The problem? At the time I didn't understand *why* I had many of those values, or even *why* I valued them. That's because some of them weren't really mine to begin with.

I realize now that some of the values were inherited from people I personally knew and respected (teachers, parents of friends, friends), while others were emulated from people in the business world I admired. Regardless, I lacked self-confidence around the values I felt were truly my own. I deserved to fully claim my own value system. I was more concerned with appeasing others or feeling accepted than standing up for what I truly believed—or even taking time to assess what it was that I believed.

After my talk with Phil, I knew I wanted to pursue something with music, but in what direction would I go with it? What kind of business would I pursue?

I was driving home from work in May 2001 when I realized local radio in Denver had pretty much shriveled up and died. There was no obituary in the papers, no funeral for friends to attend, but there was no mistake about it: Local radio was dead. DJs had stopped taking local requests, the music seemed unadventurous and burned out, all the contests involved a 1-800 number, and every radio station mysteriously went to the same programming breaks during the hour with a noticeably higher amount of commercials being aired. When I traveled, I noticed that the "local" Denver DJ also was the "local" DJ in other markets. Hmmm.

As I pulled up to the corner of Franklin Street and Exposition Avenue, I turned off the radio and officially became a disenfranchised listener, never intending to return. But, because my mind works this way, I decided to search for the cause of the slow death of local radio. If it was dead—and it was—then something had killed it.

I traced the culprit to a small provision contained on only one page inside the Telecommunications Act of 1996. Until that time, companies could own no more than forty stations nationwide and no more than two FM and two AM stations in a market. With this new law, there were no limits on how many stations companies could own nationally. Now they could own up to eight stations in a large market and up to five stations in medium markets.

Consolidation quickly ensued. Large groups took over, and radio began looking like the fast-food industry as owners made cookie-cutter, generic, homogenized programming to gain mass appeal. Every format was researched to provide a taste that was palatable to the greatest number possible, and auditorium tests provided a tight playlist of songs inside the music library to ensure the "hits" were frequently being played.

My passion for music and my desire to see a rebirth of local radio led me to Cincinnati to meet with a man recognized as a national powerhouse in radio and one of the most talented businesspeople in the entire industry. We talked for three hours and he was quite blunt.

"You'll never make it in radio in Denver," he said. "You shouldn't get into it. But if you do, here's what you need to know. You're undercapitalized, so the only properties you'll be able to buy will be broken-down stations that you'll try to make work. Rule Number 1 in radio is—and always will be—that *the power is in the tower*. The smaller stations don't have the signal strength and, therefore, are never able to grow their audience to the critical mass needed for business with national advertising agencies."

I heard the same song, in multiple verses, from numerous other people in the industry. It would be tough to break into a market where large companies already owned multiple stations and, therefore, could "cluster-sell" their advertising at average unit rates that were more competitive than I'd be able to offer. Huge radio conglomerates typically owned eight properties in the top radio markets, and they would sell a combined-stations advertising package to push down their average rates, while adding more aggregate listeners and beating their smaller competitors.

Despite the risks and challenges, I let my passion guide me and jumped into the business. I wanted success well beyond the bottom line. I hoped to build something meaningful on a company level, a business level, and a community level. I wanted stations that didn't just play music but that also made a difference in the lives of listeners and our employees. There was no stumbling. I jumped in.

However, I was entering a stark reality: I couldn't afford to buy A- or B-list broadcast properties in Denver, so I had to buy C's and D's and try to improve their signals to pick up more audience. I referred to it as "buying the ugly house on the nice block and fixing it up." It made for a riskier business model because we were buying some of the stations not based on a proven history, but on modeled predictions of how they would perform once moved to a new tower site and the transmitting power upgraded.

In September 2001, I began to meet with people in Denver who were or had been involved in the radio business. I ended up meeting a person who was a successful Denver radio veteran of thirty years. He was looking for a new opportunity and would serve as a good mentor and partner for learning the business. We attracted two other people to join our startup company, one who I knew at Cisco Systems and the other whom I had recently met when we were MBA students together at the University of Denver (a degree I elected not to finish because of the demands required in starting a new company).

We started NRC Broadcasting in February 2002, and that June we launched our first station, KNRC, which ironically wasn't a music station; it was a news/talk station, but it didn't offer a single political point of view as many major outlets now do. I intended to get beyond ideologically polarizing programming and give the audience a chance to find common ground in our increasingly divided national dialogue. We had an even amount of liberal and conservative talk show hosts who each had their own time slot throughout the week.

Frankly, it took some courage to do this kind of broadcasting. I received death threats from both sides of the political debate because people believed I was instructing our talk show hosts on what to say.

We did a lot of things right in the Denver radio market, but the large, publicly owned companies had the ratings, the most powerful transmitting signals, and the ad rates to crush us when blended with other commonly owned radio stations in Denver. The day we took KNRC off the air for lack of revenue, Clear Channel Communications switched one of its underperforming stations to the "Air America" format. They'd just been waiting to exploit the new ground that we'd tilled, and their other news/talk radio stations were already providing politically conservative and right-leaning-based programming. The reality is this type of programming shift happens a majority of the time when a programming hole opens up, but I took it personally.

The local station I owned that I was most proud of was 1510 AM, KCUV, Colorado's Underground Voice. It broadcast an excellent but not that well-known musical genre called Americana—or "roots" music—when no one else in our market was attempting such a thing. We continued to evolve the programming to also offer some tracks from the more popular contemporary-adult rock artists not being played on the bigger stations.

The further I went into the radio business and the more attention I paid to KCUV, the deeper became my attachment to music, our listeners, and the positive change I believed we were making in the Denver community. Music had significantly bolstered and improved my life when I'd needed it the most, and I now wanted to do the same thing for our audience. For the first time, my passions and my core values as a person and a consumer were all aligned. I was committed to making money, but I also truly wanted to entertain people and serve the listeners in our market on a "hyper-local" level. I was following my heart and doing something meaningful. I was getting a taste of what it was like to be in a parade for all the right reasons.

PART OF JUMPING INTO THE PARADE is being the one who seeks answers and receives input from asking the right questions. It is not being the one who is determined to make his thoughts and opinions the center of a conversation. In running the radio stations, I used my ears more than ever, especially when exploring the music and goals our local advertisers wanted to achieve. The more I listened, the more I learned about the radio business and the various advertisers that stepped up to support us. I learned about what makes people—and companies—truly tick.

I personally connected with the band Poco and its singer, Richie Furay, when he sang "Rose of Cimarron." The music and lyrics made you feel like you were sitting out with your best friends under the nighttime stars in the mountains. I understood the originality behind Derek and the Dominos' "Why Does Love Got to Be So Sad" and how Eric Clapton was uniquely singing about his own love life. I was moved more deeply every time I heard U2's "One Tree Hill" on the air, a song I had treasured since 1987. I studied chord progressions, tempos, and how to program in a way that engaged audiences, including the programming clocks and innovative ways to create new programming around advertising sponsorships.

I knew the difference between a one-hit wonder and a lasting artist. We continued to work on our recipe of songs you couldn't hear anywhere else—"deep cuts," as they are called in the business—blended with songs that had a broader appeal. It was a good balance between what the radio industry refers to as "TSL" (time spent listening) and "audience cume" (the total number of people who listen to a station). I grasped that the magic of radio really happens in between the songs, when listeners anticipate the next tune or mood shift that comes with it, and the way the DJ tees up the exit from or introduction into a music set.

At KCUV, I worked sixty-five to seventy hours a week promoting airtime that gave local artists a shot; selling advertising time; and helping with programming, engineering, and promotions, not to mention responding to all the listener feedback each day.

In Denver, we put KCUV bumper stickers on vehicles, hosted listener appreciation parties with local music bands, and offered cool T-shirts advertising the station. We built a strong independent spirit that the radio community supported; we were determined to hold our own against the invasion of "corporate radio."

At another of our Denver stations, Jack FM, we promoted "Random Jacks of Kindness," in which we paid people's parking tickets or bought their groceries or gasoline. These "Jacks of Kindness" caught on across the country and became part of other stations' community outreach. We wanted to build a legacy of empowering people and of making them passionate about radio, music, and their local community.

Our growth at NRC Broadcasting was not limited to just our efforts in Denver. Through the encouragement of our board of directors and the team from the Anschutz Corporation to which we reported, we were given the capital and support to expand our radio station ownership to thirteen radio stations in the Rocky Mountains and create hyper-local programming in the high-country ski towns. Three of our mountain stations presented college scholarships to young people, based not simply on their grade point average, but also on their community service. We gave scholarships to students who had, among other things, worked to restore Colorado's hiking trails and collected goods for an outreach program in Third World countries.

Despite all these acts of positive goodwill and all the good decisions we made in the fight to compete with the big guys, I look back now and see the confluence of other factors that began to bring us down. Yes, we were out-gunned by corporate radio, but there was nothing we could do about that. The bigger problem was this: I had jumped into this parade for all the right reasons but, over time, as the Denver stations continued to struggle, I began to doubt my own leadership abilities. I had stumbled away from the passions that had brought me to radio in the first place and began to question whether I was ever truly qualified to be the CEO. I recall thinking that any of the other CEOs of the public radio station companies, had they been in my shoes, would have been able to make the business and culture work by this point in time. They would have stopped the cash burn a long time ago, pulled the team together to all focus on the same objectives, and avoided the delays we encountered with the FCC in granting the improvements we needed to make—and would not have been sitting on poor ratings after sinking $4 million into marketing the stations. It was this "I'm not as good as everyone else" mind-set that further eroded my self-confidence and self-esteem. This negative frame of mind made me equally believe that all the things I had valued as a business leader were somehow false. That, ultimately, led to the downfall.

AS A CEO YOU MAKE HUNDREDS OF DECISIONS a day, and you only get the chance to make so many bad ones. The downfall of companies typically comes from a pattern of wrong decisions that, when combined, can become fatal.

The worst one I made at KCUV was going from AM to FM in an effort to strengthen our nighttime signal and to provide programming in the radio band where most people spent their time listening to music. At KCUV–FM, we made the decision to try to attract more listeners by taking a more mainstream artist approach, mixed with elements of the lesser-known artists that we played as an AM station. In my heart I did not have a good feeling about the programming shift, it went against my instincts, but I also felt it was important to make this decision as a team and I supported the programming shift. We steered the station's music too close to a very established radio station that had been in the market for almost thirty years. The result proved deadly because we alienated our core listening audience and failed to bring over a significant number of listeners from the heavily branded incumbent with the more powerful broadcasting signal. The first rule of radio remained: The "power is in the tower." Our ratings cratered and we never came back. We had lower ratings on FM than on AM, something that's never supposed to happen.

In August 2008 we had to pull the plug on KCUV's format. Because KCUV's signal was strong in the western suburbs of Denver and our Jack FM signal was weak in those areas, we began simulcasting the Jack FM format on both stations to reach the entire Denver metro.

Changing KCUV's format was a body blow to me personally. It brought up all the old feelings I carried about not being good enough and not belonging with the successful set. I retreated again into a victim mentality and convinced myself that I had never really deserved, or earned, the opportunity and right to be a CEO. It was simply given to me because of my father-in-law's willingness to financially back my company. Since I hadn't yet learned how to separate a feeling from an outcome, I began spiraling downward. I felt like a complete failure and that all our efforts over the past five years were for nothing.

All of this fed into the perfect storm. In August 2008, as my son and I sat up until midnight to hear KCUV play its final song before going off the air for good, the American economy was collapsing. Less than a year later, we sold off the Denver radio stations at a significant loss, but held onto twelve of the thirteen mountain stations.

The lesson I took away from all this was that no matter how hard I worked or how much I wanted something to succeed, I couldn't control everything in the business I loved: not the advertising rates, not the station ratings, and not the surrounding financial health of the nation or emerging digital media that were continuing to take market share away from traditional media. It was all outside of my ability to manage. But at the time, I hadn't learned to surrender such things, and to then reframe, adapt, and thrive without losing confidence in the internal tools that will always pull you through any situation, if you know how to use them.

Chapter 11

# Can't You Read the Signs?

> "Our humanity rests upon a series of
> learned behaviors, woven together into
> patterns that are infinitely fragile and
> never directly inherited."
>
> —*Margaret Mead*

WITH THE DEMISE OF THE RADIO STATIONS hanging over me, I started my next business, Sign Language, in 2008. I didn't launch the company from a point of passion or peace, but from anger and fear. I felt I had to show my family, my father-in-law, my business colleagues, my friends—everyone—that I could overcome the losses in radio and make this new venture work. I was going to use *my will* at any cost to my health to make this venture work. My worth as a human being and my works as a man were knotted together in ways that were not in alignment or balance.

I was still unclear on how I could ever look again in the mirror after the loss of the Denver radio stations and the invested money. I was even more puzzled how Phil could look at me, let alone speak to me. I feared I had failed him beyond repair.

He invited me to his house for a dinner between just the two of us during June 2009. It became very clear that as CEO of the radio company (which was still operating on a small scale in Denver and with our twelve stations in the mountains), I needed to completely own what had happened. Attempting to spread the blame to the board, other colleagues, or our competitors was not going to be acceptable. Phil would stand for none of that. He was honest about some of his own failings and the enormous amount of capital that went along with each failure. What mattered now, he emphasized, was how you moved forward.

"Great leaders have failures," he said. "What's most important is what you've learned from the experience and not giving up. You need to get back in, fight, and jettison what happened in the past." He clearly knew that we have a choice of what type of label we ultimately supply to an event in our lives and whether we will give failure our permission to tightly wrap itself around our talents, gifts, and strengths. Phil remained committed to standing behind me, and I believe he felt I would come around to understanding the importance of getting back into the fight.

Later in 2009 the two of us discussed how to dramatically grow Sign Language, acknowledging that it would take patience along with the right execution, and that the company would be poised for a solid market position when the economy recovered. It was at this point that I doubled or even tripled down on the bet that Sign Language could be a national player. My team put together a business plan and received the funding to build out our infrastructure and team beyond anything we had ever imagined possible one year earlier.

Our manufacturing footprint went from a five-thousand-square-foot building to a fifty-thousand-square-foot building. At the same time we made the leap of faith to embrace a "build it and they will come" model by tooling up with more printing firepower than we had customers. I made the decision to push all the chips forward on the table, and with that major capital investment there was no turning back. The entrepreneur in me couldn't resist the opportunity to build something with this much potential, and the broken ex–radio businessman in me was looking for a ticket to atonement for my recent failure.

As I ramped up Sign Language, I began to change. Instead of looking at the present and future as a new opportunity to grow internally, I settled back into my old habits of low self-esteem and a lack of self-confidence. Instead of paying heed to the advice I was given to jettison the past, I chose to compare and measure everything I was now doing in the present through the filters of my past failure. I had done absolutely nothing to learn from my experience and move on.

At KCUV, I wore jeans, T-shirts, and boots or flip-flops on non–client-facing days. At Sign Language, I began donning suits, ties, and cufflinks. I joined a number of professional organizations and various boards of directors. It was as if a light switch had gone on, and I now was pretending to be a powerful CEO by trying to play a role in a drama I didn't write. I continued to come up with new reasons why I had failed in the radio business. My rationale at the time was that I had been too casual and relaxed, and that successful business leaders conducted themselves differently. Any win we had at Sign Language was always overshadowed by my perceived failures with the Denver radio stations. We built Sign Language from the ground up, and we gradually earned success, but I kept pushing for some greater statement of atonement. With Sign Language, I was determined to prove to the world that I was smart enough, good enough, and capable enough to be taken seriously as a senior executive. To this end, I began joining boards so I could be very visible and be around people who had "made it," emulating their values, even if they weren't fully my own.

One and a half years after launching Sign Language, Libby looked at me and said, "Who are you? What have you become?"

SOMETIMES AS I WAS DRIVING around Denver in between sales calls for Sign Language, I'd glance toward the Rockies and have these mini–"Glory Days" type of moments. I would think about how I'd managed to get the last FM broadcast signal installed on Lookout Mountain on Colorado's Front Range. That's where my heart was—still up in that tower. But when KCUV disintegrated, I no longer felt compelled to follow my dreams and continued to convince myself that the problem was with me personally.

One evening, my son, who was seven at the time, came to me and asked, "What's wrong, Daddy?" I told him about some of the economic and company problems and said, "I'm working as hard as I can right now because I want to make you and Mom proud of me, and Sign Language is still struggling to get new customers." The next morning he left me a note that he'd written the night before: "To Dad—to help with your cumpny [sic]." Accompanying the note was a $10 bill from his piggy bank.

I was moved beyond expression (the sawbuck and the note now share a frame that sits on the mantel over my fireplace), and I kept working even harder, ignoring all the gathering signs of personal trouble.

The costs were accumulating within me—but so were the profits. While I was dying inside, we were growing the business. We printed a grand total of fifty 14′ × 48′ billboard vinyls in 2010, but in September 2011, our momentum continued to build and we produced a thousand by the third week of September, setting a new monthly record. We grew because we made a conscious decision to stop acting like a printing company and start acting like an outdoor advertising company.

Our commitment to being different from other printers included learning the business cycles of our customers. Outdoor billboard companies receive a lot of orders at the end of the month, and most want to get everything posted for their customers by the beginning of the next month. Printing companies, however, always pushed to get everything done by the end of the month. We adjusted our printing schedules to line up with the sales cycles of the outdoor advertising companies. By shifting our direction and adopting our customers' schedules, we turned around our cash flow within six months.

We started to listen intently to our customers so that we understood their challenges. Listening, really listening, forced us to focus on our customers' challenges instead of worrying about ourselves. In doing so, we became a more integrated partner, and they began trusting us and sending more business our way, including new areas of outdoor advertising like wallscapes and transit applications.

The tool behind our growth was simple: Be flexible. The definition of our success? When Plan B works. You don't have to invent something, just innovate it. We did just that, and our entire team moved collectively in that direction. "Service driven, by design" became our brand and the key to our success. Unfortunately, I hadn't adopted that motto across all the areas of my life. It was business, not personal.

NOTHING ABOUT THE TRANSFORMATION in my life has been easy, but all of it has been enormously worthwhile. Everyone has heard Woody Allen's famous quote, "Eighty percent of success is just showing up." Well, jumping into the parade is not about just showing up. It's about breaking out of that pattern so we can live differently on a daily basis. It's about being willing to do the work and complete the process.

In some ways, I had one foot in the parade already, but that wasn't nearly enough to prevent what was coming. I didn't handle the pressure of all that was crumbling around me in my personal life, and it nearly cost me everything. Instead, I found hope. The troubles of life didn't fade away, but I discovered a path that includes joy, regardless of the highs or lows. I began to build spiritual muscle and to live with a purpose. It was then that I truly jumped into the parade.

Chapter 12

# Living into Alignment

"Faith is taking the first step even when
you can't see the whole staircase."

—*Martin Luther King, Jr.*

A S PART OF BUILDING SPIRITUAL MUSCLE, my coach,
Stephen McGhee, recommended that I watch *Seven
Days in Utopia*, a movie about a golfer who learns about
faith, purpose, and how to be true to yourself. Critics
panned the movie when it came out in 2011, but I watched
it with my son, and it brought me to tears. It was one of
the most important films I've ever seen, coming at exactly
the right moment for me to receive it in December 2011,
only three weeks after the Bentley incident.

During one scene, the main character is told to make a
list of all the lies he's told about himself, all the lies people
have told about him, and all the truths he knows about
himself. He puts the lies in a box and buries it, keeping
the truths with him.

So in April 2012, I hiked with my Young Presidents'
Organization (YPO) forum members to Phantom Ranch
at the bottom of the Grand Canyon and buried my own

box of lies. When the seven of us arrived at the ranch, I went off on my own, walking in the isolation and quiet of the massive canyon until I found a spot near a little finger that comes off the Colorado River. Using my hands and a stick from the desert floor, I dug a hole and buried all the lies others had told about me and all the lies that I'd told about myself—that I was unworthy of being a father to my son, that I'd failed in the radio business, that I didn't belong in successful circles in Denver society, that I didn't deserve to be loved and accepted simply for who I am. I put all these lies and more in the ground for good and covered the gravesite with rocks.

Standing at the bottom of the Grand Canyon, I made a commitment that I knew I was going to keep: The lies were going to stop. They were dead. Buried. I couldn't control what others said about me, but I didn't have to believe their lies. And I could take charge of the harmful and hurtful things I'd too often said about myself.

I had used an imaginative tool and taken a conscious and active step away from the past and toward the unknown future. This painful and in some ways unsettling step was yet another step out of my comfort zone. Libby and I had separated two months prior to this trip, and I was adjusting to life on my own at a time when I still didn't do "alone" very well. And while the lies were, well, lies, they had provided a certain comfort. They were my crutch, my excuse, my security blanket, my comfortable way around the truths that I wanted to avoid. They were the fun-loving roommate who kept me company and told me what I wanted to hear and somehow got me to overlook the fact that he didn't pay his share of the rent or clean up after himself.

This is the nature of brokenness. It's living in a self-imposed bondage to lies because you've become comfortable with those lies and fear the truth, even when the truth is the only thing that can ever set you free. So as I took my lies to the bottom of the Grand Canyon, there was a part of me that didn't want to leave them there—a part of me, that dark part whispering in my ear, that said I couldn't live without them.

The effect of the burial, however, was incredible. It taught me something I continue to learn over and over again: True growth and genuine joy often occur outside my comfort zone.

Walking back to join my YPO forum-mates that afternoon, I felt incredibly peaceful and light. When we hiked out of the canyon the next day, I traveled with a much lighter load. Ridding myself of all those lies was like dumping a backpack full of rocks from my shoulders. I found myself racing up the canyon. I felt connected to a different purpose, a higher one somehow, even though I couldn't have said what it was. All I knew from my heart was that if I trusted this impulse and truly followed it, something new would come.

It was an important step toward what I call "living into alignment," which is the point behind developing all that spiritual muscle.

When we live into alignment, we no longer randomly stumble into the next phase of life. Instead, we take ownership of our core values and align those values throughout every area of our life: in our faith, with our family, with our friends, at our work, as a philanthropist, with someone we've just met . . . in all our roles as a human being. When we are living into alignment, we can jump

into the parade for all the right reasons and truly make
a difference in the world. We can live with purpose and
meaning.

WHEN I RETURNED TO DENVER from my Grand Canyon
trip, I began using another tool for building more spiritual muscle that would help me live into alignment: the
tool of investing in others. Within a few days of every
meeting with a prospective business partner, employer,
client, trusted friend, or new relationship, I sat down and
handwrote a letter to that person.

The letters went beyond a "thank you" and went
beyond a recap of the meeting. With each letter, I did my
best to really listen and then mirror back to them how
I heard they were navigating the unique challenges and
victories of their own lives. I searched my heart for ways
to connect in personal, transparent, and genuine ways.
It was a personal discovery of how I could serve others
differently, and it felt, and feels, incredible.

The act of putting words on paper made me clarify
what I really wanted to say in a manner I'd never experienced before. Like so many exercises that bring health and
healing, this one felt like a risk. I was sharing parts of me
that these people had never heard, pushing the conversation to a deeper, more personal level when appropriate. I
had no idea how they would react to it, and I had initial
apprehensions of being judged for crossing a "human"
line in what in most cases had been strictly professional
relationships.

Surprisingly, nearly every letter led to a deeper business connection, but, more importantly, each led to
a deeper spiritual connection as well. The people who
received the notes often wrote, called, or emailed me back

and revealed their own desire for a greater sense of connectedness. I wasn't the only one who'd gone through hard times or still struggled with ghosts from the past.

I discovered how challenges and adversity in life connect us all because they're something we all share. More vulnerability led to more openness, which led to more meaningful communication, which led to more creativity. I was uncovering the correlation between my increased humility and my expanding world.

For years I saw my vulnerability as a liability, but through this new process of transparency, I began to see it as a source of strength for me and empathy for others; it is an asset for opening doors into living and leadership. Sharing my story and hearing so many compelling stories from other people helped me discover that the unknown produces the unexpected, and that the unexpected life was the one I was after. Before, I had viewed anything unexpected as an unwelcome and negative surprise, not as a gift.

It also was a way of serving others rather than just serving me. I no longer was *thinking* about reaching out to others, but actively taking a step in that direction.

AS I BUILT MORE SPIRITUAL MUSCLE, I took more and more steps of action toward others from a place of gratitude and service. This was something I identified as a core value I could own and integrate into all areas of my life. It would become a central tenet to living into alignment, and it helped me connect not only to other people but to God.

When I had my Denver radio stations, the standard I set for myself was all about a call to action—"You've got to get out there and get it done"—with a singular focus on my career. Living into alignment is not focused on the action so much, but is all about the call to service, where you're simultaneously exposing and building the potential of others and yourself. So I took ownership of "serving others" as a value. It became mine, and I made a commitment to living it in all areas of my life. I committed to aligning my life around the value of serving.

A call to serviceable action is something that benefits other people. It also benefits God. And, last of all, it will benefit the one doing it (me and you), in part because it helps connect us to God. I learned this in a unique way when I began weekly tithing of what, to me, is a large sum of money to my church and other nonprofits. Giving more than 10 percent of my income each week, sometimes anonymously, has an impact on the lives of people I don't know and comes back to me in ways I often don't understand or even know.

As my life has become aligned with my purpose of service, my self-esteem has grown in new and unexpected ways. One of those ways involves how I interact with God. For decades, I'd gone to church, but I'd only just thought about God. It hadn't occurred to me that one very good tool to use before approaching God was to take the time to define my values—not just in business, but in every part of my life. A key piece of living into alignment, I now realized, was that I had to find my own way to relate to God. I couldn't metaphorically pick up my father's religious clothes and put them on. They didn't fit my body or my soul, and nothing I could do would make them conform to me. I wasn't rejecting anyone else's path, just seeking my own. I had to come with my values; no one else's. And I truly had to understand the "why" behind choosing those values. No one could define that for me, and I believe no one can define it for you.

Here's another example of how this changed the way I lived. For years I'd prayed for God to let me do well in a sales call because we really needed the money for our company. A successful transaction in the marketplace would generate revenue for us and obviously be beneficial. It took a while, and quite a lot of pain, before I grasped that those were one-way, self-centered requests. Anyone in business obviously wants his or her company to succeed. The difference now is that I pray to God for wisdom and knowledge to perform my best, surrender, and leave the rest to Him.

I used to lead from force and from a misplaced faith in control, not from faith in empowerment and being empowered. I had plenty of *head* knowledge from everything my father-in-law and other mentors had taught me, but I didn't have their *heart* knowledge because I hadn't jumped into the parade for the right reasons.

The unaligned life centers on trying to ensure survival and thinking tactically about how to do that. Living into alignment is about having a long-range strategy to get beyond the survival mentality and into something more expansive and creative. The difference between focusing on tactics and focusing on strategy is the difference between managing and leading, between existing and thriving, between being in neutral and growing.

Jumping into the parade is all about exploring uncharted waters. We have to trust the process and be gentle on ourselves when the timing takes longer than we expect, or we'll second-guess ourselves into nonexistence.

Again, this is the difference between management and life leadership. Management focuses on what already exists, on making those things work as well as possible, and on trying to improve those things. Life leadership focuses on things that don't exist and creates them—in others as well as in ourselves. Jumping into the parade is about following that something inside of us that wants to come into existence. It is up to each of us to create our own experience, our day, and our life. It's up to us to discover the joy that awaits us in life.

I COULD NEVER GET BEYOND MY PAST until I stopped everything I was doing long enough to confront my ghosts in a more honest and organized way. After returning to Denver from New York following the most difficult night of my life, I consciously set out to leave behind my comfort zone and examine the experiences and the fears that had shaped my childhood (and most of my adulthood). I stopped defending myself and stopped rationalizing what I was supposed to think or feel. I let myself feel all the pain and all the shame that had been festering within me since I was a boy. It was my first step in starting over and toward living into alignment.

We have the power to turn adversity into life opportunities, and I remind myself of that daily.

I recognize that owning my values and living them out in all areas of my life will allow me to live successfully, because it takes failure out of the equation. Oh, things could go wrong—they have and they always will. But those things don't steal my joy; they no longer define who I am or my value as a person.

The key to living into alignment is to let our senses and our hearts guide us. We have to trust the smallest messages that speak to us when we're genuinely quiet and receptive, willing to listen to what our spirits are trying to teach us. It's our spirits that create the connective glue between the physical, mental, emotional, and social parts of us.

It teaches us that fear isn't our adversary, but our ally and our teacher. It's a gift—if we're willing to receive it in the appropriate way and cooperate with it to bring about change.

Chapter 13

# Growing the Big "S"

"Be careful how you live. You may be
the only Bible some person ever read."

—*William Toms*

WHEN THE STATE OF COLORADO CUT FUNDING for
its suicide prevention hotline and other mental
health programs in 2011, Joe Conrad was one of the few
people who actively stepped in to help fill the void.

Joe is the founder and CEO of Cactus, a large advertising agency in Denver. He and his company led the efforts
to create Man Therapy, a clever web-based program that
provides men with resources for dealing with depression
and other challenges of life.

Joe had no idea of the personal struggles I was going
through when we had breakfast at Racines in early 2011
and he shared the vision for the Man Therapy project. I was
on the board of the Anschutz Foundation at the time, so he
was simply seeking advice on how to gain support for the
startup nonprofit. His company was doing the work pro
bono, but there were additional hard costs and he needed
funding partners. I helped arrange the introduction, and

the foundation ultimately decided to offer seed funding to help Joe get the project up and running.

Joe's team at Cactus eventually created a campaign and program around Dr. Rich Mahogany, a fictional front man for the Man Therapy website. Dr. Mahogany—picture *Anchorman*'s Ron Burgundy, but as a therapist—would cut through the stigma and become the go-to expert for men struggling with issues when they no longer had access to social services.

It may surprise you to know that working-age men (twenty-five to fifty-four years old) account for the largest number of suicide deaths in Colorado. These men are also the least likely to receive any kind of support. We don't talk about it with our friends. We don't share it with our families. And we sure as heck don't seek professional treatment. And as Dr. Rich Mahogany is the first to say, we are the victims of problematic thinking that says mental health disorders are *unmanly* signs of weakness.

As you might imagine, the project became even more personal a few months later after my experience at the Bentley. Although I kept my experience in New York to myself, many of the people working on the Man Therapy project didn't have the kind of firsthand experience with a psychological crisis that I'd had, so I felt that I could make a contribution. I gave small input to the various concepts and donated the printing for the production set used in videos that became part of the program in 2012.

As I went about the process of building spiritual muscle, I got more involved in the project. My father-in-law, as well as the foundation's executive director, continued to support me in raising money for the development of Man Therapy and for the outdoor advertising expenses we used to promote the initial launch. It was highly rewarding to watch the concept quickly catch fire and grow; now it's being considered for use in the United States outside Colorado, and was launched in Australia in 2013.

The resources of Man Therapy weren't available to me in the months leading up to my decision point at the elevator of the Bentley, but I'm glad they're now available to other men. And while I no longer work with the program because it became too emotionally draining, the time I spent on it played a key role in the reconstruction of my life.

Working on projects like Man Therapy has been one of the most important tools in building spiritual muscle, because it helped me move away from the "self" (small "s") and toward the "Self" (big "S").

The small "s" is the ego-centered part of the self. It's selfishness personified. It leads and lives based on fear, because its goal is to win the approval of others and nab all the credit. It's driven in large part by pop culture's emphasis on doing what "feels right" at the time, rather than committing to the long-term good.

The big "S" is selflessness personified, because it's about our connection to God and serving a larger purpose. It trusts the process of life, and it leads and lives based on uncovering who we really are and then being true to that Self. This process is not a sprint, but a marathon, and we start the race by putting God first, others second, and ourselves third. And even though it's focused on others, it brings joy. One Christian friend put it this way: Joy is an acronym for this order—Jesus, Others, Yourself.

In business leadership, "1 + 1 = Unlimited" is about letting go of control and being smart enough to check our egos at the door so we can surround ourselves with people who are smarter than us. Our job is to create an environment that allows them to thrive; we're a macro-manager, not a micro-manager. By empowering others and trusting them, we'll build something much greater.

To trust and empower others—in business and in life—we must willingly break the fundamentally destructive habit of judging. The small "s" judges yourself and others, but the big "S" doesn't need to justify or rationalize anything. It's all-accepting and all-loving.

I've come to enjoy the peace that this acceptance brings. I was always my toughest critic and would berate myself constantly to perform and live up to a standard that was never possible. There was always a carryover from this attitude to other people; they paid a price for my insecurities. When we stop judging others, and ourselves, we're free to serve sincerely and selflessly—little "s," not big.

IN PART because of the lessons I learned from working with Phil, I was less drawn to raising money for the arts and more to helping people who were suffering and required basic and advanced human needs. Phil believes that we all possess the ability to help restore and influence a person's self-esteem and confidence by seemingly small acts of kindness. It's something he taught me not just through his words, but by the way he lived and gave to others around him.

"Do good work quietly," he said. "When you do that, you gain as much or more than the people you're serving."

This approach fit me well because it addressed some of the pain and shame I'd experienced growing up. In the summer of 1988, I spent the first three weeks following my freshman year with a college friend, because, frankly, I had nowhere else to go. I slept at his house, ate with his family, and pretty much made myself at home. When my friend got a job at a summer camp in Estes Park, Colorado, I went with the family to drop him off. On the way back, we stopped at a McDonald's in Boulder, Colorado. We were standing in line when my friend's father turned to his wife and said, "I guess I have to buy Tim's dinner again."

I was hungry, but I looked at my friend's mother and said, "I'm fine. I'm not hungry."

I felt tremendous shame hearing him say that in front of my friend's mother and two younger brothers, not to mention everyone else within earshot. I felt like a low-life, and it only strengthened my resolve to break from my dependence on others. I also determined on that day never to make people feel ashamed of their circumstances. So when I was doing charity work through the Anschutz Foundation, I always gravitated toward projects of human needs—restoring people's dignity, trying to give them faith in an outcome.

For instance, during my interactions with various nonprofits I kept hearing about the horrendous problems associated with methamphetamine. I reached out to the Colorado Meth Project in 2010, was accepted to its board of directors, and helped with some of its incredible community outreach initiatives, including an awareness campaign that included billboards with supporting radio and TV ads. I also traveled to Washington, DC, with Kent MacLennan, the executive director of the program in Colorado, to meet with senators and congressmen from Colorado. Our goal was to get more federal funding, in addition to foundation funding, to fight the growing number of meth addicts in our state.

This type of philanthropic work not only allowed me to give back to others, but it also let me use some of the most painful experiences of my early life for a positive purpose. We can't change the past, but we can accept it and forgive it and put it to work in ways we could never have imagined when we were young.

The more I've been involved in these efforts, and the more they've given back to me, the more value I've seen in the compassion and empathy I developed from growing up with my mother. All of us have life experiences that contribute to our effectiveness in reaching and helping others, because all of us relate to messages differently. We can hear a message several times from different people and never "get it" until we finally hear it from that one person who shares it from just the right perspective that connects to our own experiences. The lightbulb goes on, and we finally internalize the message and grow.

My experiences with my mother helped me develop empathy for many of the things she experienced. The vulnerability I'd known as a child had taught me about substance abuse and the need for compassion when dealing with addiction. I saw up close what drug and alcohol abuse can do, and I was now committed to making a difference in the lives of those fighting these problems. Very often, I find myself connecting to people largely because my background somehow connects to theirs. And that brings me great joy.

WHEN I SEE LEADERS working with people with the most desperate of needs, it brings me hope in every way, helps clarify my own values, and shows me a side of people I often don't get to see in the business world. You don't really know people until you see them with their sleeves rolled up and their hands dirty, sacrificing their time and energy for something larger than themselves.

Don Gallegos, the former CEO of the grocery chain King Soopers, immediately comes to mind as I think about this. He has made Father Woody's Haven of Hope one of the nonprofits he supports with his time and capital contributions. It is not an overnight shelter, but rather a place where the indigent and homeless can go to get a hot meal, take a shower, do their laundry, have their mail sent, and make their phone calls—but most of all, restore their dignity. Most importantly, it is driven by its motto, "We are here to serve, not to judge." This powerful ex-CEO does just that. He now devotes himself to helping people living on the street. He's not only there offering his assistance, but he also uses his business expertise to negotiate contracts which provide food for them that would normally get thrown away.

Leaders like Don inspire me to get involved and serve others, which always ends up making my life better as well. When we're serving others, there's no time to focus on our worries or stress. In a very tangible way, we get more from what we give.

When we give to others from the attitude of the big "S," the pot is infinite and the rewards are there for everyone.

THE BENEFITS OF DEVELOPING the big "S" of selflessness don't just show up when we do service projects. It's a force in the business world as well.

There are times in business when we have to lay aside our little "s" (our selfish ego) and deal with immediate problems that can turn into much bigger troubles. For business leaders, it's often uncomfortable to call people out when they're being disruptive inside the organization. Helping them understand their destructive behavior, however, is a major part of a leader's job. It's equally important to call people out when they do things right, and it's hard to do that if you're wrapped up in the little "s" of selfishness. Your attachment to ego won't let you spread the credit. The big "S" shares the credit.

At Sign Language, I regularly walked the halls and talked with our salespeople and those running the printers on the production facility floor. I made a point of interacting with them daily, even when other things might have been more pressing.

"Things haven't been this bad for the American economy since the 1930s," I told them. "But our company has grown from one employee to sixty in our printing operation, while we've almost doubled or at times more than doubled our revenue every single year. You're the ones responsible for driving this expansion."

Whenever I made these types of comments, I thought about the decades it had taken me to discover the true meaning of the word "self." The results of this small shift within me were tangible within the business itself. At Sign Language, we had incredible employees. We took risks together with the purpose and goal of serving others. And we all led together—the hallmark of a great organization.

I left Sign Language in January 2013 because I personally felt the need to make a career change and do things that were less directly connected to my former father-in-law. It was a hard decision, in part because things were going really well financially and because I loved the people I worked with and worked for. God had redeemed a situation that I'd started out of fear and anger into an organization I was leading out of passion and joy. Because of that, I was taking a lot of good memories with me when I left.

On my last day at Sign Language, Jeff Shumaker, our COO, put the names and pictures of all of our employees and their families on a wall about fifty feet long. He said, "I want you to see the names and pictures of all the lives you've impacted that you didn't realize you were affecting."

Pure joy.

WHENEVER I START TO SPIRAL INWARD and focus only on my own problems, I actively shift the focus to other people. I think about them. I pray for them or reach out and make contact through calling, writing, meeting, or walking with them. That seemingly small step can change everything.

I keep a list of all of the people who are important to me in a drawer by my nightstand. Whenever I start to feel a little down, I pull out the list and study it. I begin praying for them or sending them emails that simply say, "How are you? You were on my mind." Sometimes on my walks I send a text to a person and say something personal like, "I went by our old school and had a memory of the two of us throwing a football in the field."

These small, sustainable, daily gestures make up the steps that can take us into a new way of living. They lead to a sustainability of Self, with the big "S," which keeps you connected to God and others in more ways than you might expect at first. Like business, life is multifaceted, not focused around just one piece of our identity or one role that we play in society, where our purpose appears limited.

Chapter 14

# The Birth of Heart Wisdom

*"It is not my ability, but my response to God's ability that counts."*

—*Corrie ten Boom*

AS I CONTINUED TO BUILD my spiritual muscle by expressing my gratitude, burying my lies, and starting the process of forgiveness, I started to notice a subtle change in how I was functioning in the world. I stopped analyzing and began listening more deeply to myself as I relied on my heart to guide me and move me forward.

So rather than just *thinking* something like, "I will be used for a larger purpose," I started getting in touch with parts of me that I'd long undervalued or neglected. When I listened to my heart, I naturally served others. My heart and my actions were finally aligning. Things I couldn't resolve through analytics were accepted and embraced through the wisdom of my heart.

I hadn't left logic behind. There's nothing wrong with using logic and good information to make good decisions. That's smart. Logic, information, data, knowledge, analysis . . . it's all important. But those things are simply tools in our toolbox. Heart wisdom, I discovered, allows us to use those tools the right way.

In some ways, this transformation came naturally as a result of the exercises I was doing to develop spiritual muscle. But I found I was still struggling to truly understand heart wisdom. And the most challenging thing about heart wisdom, I learned, is that it's not a tool you can pick up at a local store. In fact, it's not a *thing* at all—it's a *process* and a *knowing*.

During the first few months following my experience in New York, I began to do the hard work needed to build my spiritual muscle. But I made the mistake of thinking I'd *arrived*. My life was different, but I soon realized that I hadn't come to the end of the line; it was just a part of the journey.

The journey—yours and mine—involves a never-ending process of making our way through life, stumbling at times, and learning the life lessons that turn all our intellectual knowledge into something of real value: heart wisdom. We develop that type of wisdom during the pauses—the "in-between" phases of life, as some have called it—and then gently apply it as we keep on living. In many cases, these pauses provide the deepest value to our lives, more value than the action itself. Those pauses give us the *knowing*, not the doing.

My marriage provided the most powerful example I can think of to illustrate this point. When Libby and I began dating, I had no trouble following my heart. I didn't need to put the pros and cons on paper. I knew I wanted to marry her. I listened to my heart. And even though the marriage didn't survive, ending in August 2012, we experienced tremendous blessings along the way. We had

a son together, of course, but that was just one of the
blessings that came from our marriage.

During our twelve years of marriage, and in the time
since, I truly began to understand the power of heart
wisdom. Much of that heart wisdom actually came as a
result of our struggles.

Not long after we returned from our honeymoon, her
dad shared some great advice about protecting my marriage from the destructive forces that inevitably would
come between us: the demands of our careers, the lure
of false ideals, friends with different values. I received an
immense amount of wisdom from him about the journey
of marriage, but I didn't have the experiences to fully
grasp all that he was sharing with me at the time. It was
head knowledge and wasted wisdom. And while I put a
great deal of head knowledge into trying to solve the various challenges we faced in our marriage, I simply lacked
the heart wisdom—or the *knowing*—to pull us through
some harder times.

I've since discovered that once we begin living into
alignment with our values and believing in faith, the wisdom of our heart, our life experiences begin to shape that
wisdom. Then we begin to see more clearly how we are
best able to apply the things we know.

Failure is an important part of the process of developing heart wisdom. If we let ourselves get in the victim
mind-set, as I so often have over the years, we never truly
learn. We pass the buck, make excuses, and blame everything and everybody but ourselves.

I got into the radio business against the advice of
many people who were accomplished and successful radio
industry veterans, but it was a heart decision. While my

colleagues and I had our share of trials and tribulations, I don't ever regret getting into that business. Then I got into the printing business—partly out of anger and fear and feeling like I had to prove myself, but partly because printing fascinated me. I felt drawn to it in my heart. I didn't know much more than how to operate a desktop printer, but I somehow knew I'd love the printing business. And I did.

My real mistakes always came when I stopped following my heart and started beating myself up for the failures that simply were part of my learning process. I had yet to realize that life is one long and wonderful learning opportunity, where there is no such thing as failure, only experiences. I often was so blinded by trying to atone for the family I was born into and trying to prove myself to others that I gave myself no grace or ever asked myself what opportunities might come from the experience. I would berate myself and second-guess myself into oblivion, and then I'd go right back to my old ways: trying to appease others and prove myself to others rather than embracing all the value of the lessons I had learned.

It's not always easy to love yourself—all the parts of yourself—in a non-narcissistic type of way, but that's what it takes. If we don't learn to love and accept ourselves, we're always in danger of going back to our old ways. To develop heart wisdom and a true knowing, we have to love ourselves for our failures, for our successes, and, most importantly, for the things we have yet to learn.

God can help us learn from everything that happens in life, though sometimes we don't embrace the lessons or see the good that can come out of it until a while down the road. It's during the difficult periods—the in-between phases—that we learn the most. That's when we have to apply faith to an outcome we can't necessarily see.

George Müller, a well-known Prussian evangelist of the nineteenth century, once said, "Faith does not operate in the realm of the possible. There is no glory for God in that which is humanly possible. Faith begins where man's power ends." And he didn't just say it, he lived it. Müller never took a salary as director of the New Orphan Houses in Bristol, England, and he never asked for donations to that cause, yet he built a campus that served more than ten thousand orphans.

In perhaps the most famous example of his faith, Müller once gave thanks for breakfast even though he had nothing to feed the children. As he closed his prayer, there was a knock on the door. A baker had decided to bring by some fresh bread, and a milkman's cart had broken down right in front of the orphanage. Müller didn't know how his prayers would be answered that morning, but he never lacked faith that God would provide.

Müller's faith defies logic. Logic persuades us to play it safe, to avoid the risks of life rather than trust in God's plan. Faith begins when we realize we can't think our way out of our dilemmas and painful situations and we begin to trust in a plan greater than ourselves.

When we become quiet and listen to the pauses during the in-between pieces of our lives, we can hear our hearts and the heart wisdom that frees us to actually begin living.

I AM COMING TO TERMS with something a friend shared with me two years ago: We're all "imperfectly perfect." Accepting that has freed me to listen to my heart wisdom because it allows me to accept that I'm always changing and, hopefully, improving. There is no state of perfection. I never have to get to a state of being in total alignment; rather, I'm always in the *process* of living into alignment.

Starting that cycle isn't easy. Our minds can rationalize anything, justify anything, and convince us of anything. So we have to work to trust our heart—a muscle that is creative, intuitive, and grounded in a truth that's born of our shared experiences. The very idea of trusting heart wisdom can seem counterintuitive, but allow me to share some areas in which trusting heart wisdom has helped me live with more faith and joy.

First, heart wisdom helps develop authentic spiritual muscle. As a young adult, I would have said I had a lot of spiritual muscle. I'd followed the trappings of religion: I'd gone to church, tried to be a believer, and convinced myself that my relationship with God was solid.

It wasn't until I found myself living in a state of crisis that I realized I was rationalizing and not feeling. My relationship with God went one way: with me asking God for things I wanted and not listening to what He said I needed. There's a big difference between what we think we want and what we actually need, and it's the difference between relying on the head instead of the heart.

Second, heart wisdom creates a more decisive leader and caring person. When we are facing a decision and gathering the facts, our head often presents counterarguments to each and every position. Our heart, however, knows the score. It doesn't waffle on truth. When is the truth not the truth? The heart knows the answer: never.

The more we trust our heart wisdom, the quicker we make decisions. We can enter unexpected situations with unknown variables and make sound decisions in seconds.

Third, heart wisdom helps relationships with other people. The heart doesn't need to control other people because it knows we're never going to control another person. The best we can hope for is to influence another person's life in a positive way. By embracing this, we also make it a simple decision to determine who we want to surround ourselves with on a daily basis.

This hit home for me following my divorce, when I realized that more than half the people in the photos on my "wall of friends" hadn't reached out to me at all since I had moved out of the house with Libby. People going through a divorce need family and friends in their lives, just as they would during any other loss. A loved one hasn't died, but it's the death of a significant relationship, and they need people around them to comfort them as they grieve. The fact that a number of "friends" of mine didn't show up—their actions spoke for themselves—was actually a relief. I value people who value me, and from this experience I dramatically pared down the number of people I invest time in and with.

Fourth, heart wisdom generates authentic forgiveness. There's a difference between forgiveness and reconciliation. Reconciliation is something we sometimes have to do, and it requires two people. Forgiveness only takes one person, and we do it to move on with our lives. When people hurt us, it's like the bite of a rattlesnake. We can choose to dwell on the poison from the bite or expunge it and move on with our lives. The reality is that a snake is a snake, and it has since gone on to bite more people and has completely forgotten about ever biting us.

Until we actually let ourselves feel the full impact of forgiveness from the heart, we won't be able to move on and rebuild. As I continue to learn to forgive myself, I am freed to forgive others, and once I begin forgiving others, I am free to experience joy more fully.

Fifth, heart wisdom makes us meek—and strong. People who are selfless (the big "S") and in touch with their hearts will know the real joys and riches around them. They will be fulfilled by relationships, by feeling love, by being accepted, and by living a life of peace in their hearts. Contrary to popular belief, meek means powerful.

This goes against everything that our head, our ego, and much of our society tell us, because we want to put ourselves first, not other people's interests. The greater truths come when we listen to the heart and it says, "This is not all about me. It's about serving. The more I serve, the more filled I am."

Sixth, heart wisdom is healthy. When we live with heart wisdom and in forgiveness, we breathe freely. And breathing freely is a great source for improving our mental, physical, and emotional health. Why are antianxiety drugs some of the most prescribed medications in the country? Because when the head and heart are in conflict, the friction creates tremendous doubt, worry, and fear. Heart wisdom aligns the head and the heart to live with the courage that's born of faith.

It's all about getting clear on who you are and what you want out of life. I continue to choose to stop putting myself into situations that don't bring me joy. I was constantly doing things because I thought I needed to be visible. I began sleeping a lot better when I removed these events from my life, as well as when I started investing in the right people. Another example is hunting. I once loved to hunt, but being around guns now brings me anxiety. I hope that lifts completely someday, as I would love to hunt again. The point here is that I finally had to come clean with some of my friends who were always inviting me to go hunting, instead of having my "excuse de jour" on why I couldn't join them.

Seventh, and finally, heart wisdom drives out fear and takes advantage of pain. Fear comes from the head and pain comes from the heart. Fear wants to paralyze us, while pain helps us make clearer decisions.

When I feel pain in my heart I'm alerted to my deepest needs. The heart uses pain to get our attention. That's how heart knowledge knows the difference between right and wrong: because there's no pain when things are right.

When we honestly confront an issue and live from the heart, our heart is in sync with our brain, the world opens up, and we have greater clarity and purpose. People around us feel this and are attracted to that special sense of an extraordinary leader—not just a leader in the business world, but a life leader. And the strange and funny thing is that we become extraordinary life leaders by doing things that are very ordinary. We are just doing them repetitively, step by step and day by day. Through this process we build spiritual muscle and sustainable action, as we learn to live into alignment. We can live a very remarkable life by just listening to our hearts.

Chapter 15

# The Power of Clarity

"People who say it cannot be done
should not interrupt those who are
doing it."

—*George Bernard Shaw*

I N OCTOBER 2013, I sat down with pen and paper and peered into my heart. The time had come for me to begin thinking about the possibility of someday sharing my life with another person again. I thought long and hard about the commitments I would make to that person, and whether I could recommit to those commitments if and when I found that special person.

"I want to be filled in my soul, heart, and mind differently," I wrote, "and I realize that this all begins with clarity around the character traits I value—in both my future wife and myself."

Based on all that I had learned up to that point in my life—the combination of heart wisdom and head knowledge—I created a list of values that I knew I would commit to fully, things like unconditional love, acceptance, forgiveness, and actions that line up with our words.

When I look back at the "personal commitments" I wrote down that day, I realize they reflect the values I've been referencing throughout this book. Some are specific to a marriage relationship, like "fidelity to her in mind, body, and soul with no exceptions" or "being there through the good and the bad." Others are more general, like "living with courage and not allowing myself to be limited by fear" or "doing the right thing when no one is watching."

There's tremendous power in that list, because, as I've come to learn, there's tremendous power in clarity.

Some of the worst periods of my life are marked by common threads of chaos and confusion, where clarity was in short supply. I wasn't in tune with the wisdom of my heart, and I wasn't living into alignment with my values. Why? I didn't lack information or resources. I had money and capabilities. I knew the right people. I had energy. What I lacked was clarity.

I lived in a self-created haze and, as a result, I listened to a number of different people and focused on their often misguided information. And, worst of all, I tried to control situations and outcomes. I lived as a victim—doubting myself, blaming everyone, and never seeking truth unless it fit my needs at the time. When I couldn't control things, I grew angry and frustrated in my impatience.

I've had moments of clarity throughout my life, but nothing like the transformative clarity that came after I pushed the Down button on that hotel elevator in New York. It's not that everything became crystal clear at that moment, but that moment opened my eyes and gave me a fresh vision for my life, a new hope for my future.

So as I began building spiritual muscle, a new thread emerged: clarity.

We're all here for a reason, so it's important that we really know what we want out of life—in our family lives, our friendships, our spiritual lives, and our business lives. It is no accident that as we get older, time appears to speed up. My reasoning for this is that we have more clarity around how much time we've used and how much time we have left, and have come to terms with our own mortality and the unknown future ahead. As I emerged from the chaos I helped create in my former life, I began to develop clarity around my values, which led to clarity around the things I wanted out of life, around the people I wanted in (or out of) my life, around my relationship with my son, and around my relationship with God. And I now have the growing clarity to know that being true to myself starts, and finishes, with living into alignment across all aspects of my life.

This type of clarity begins by following the heart, as I mentioned in the previous chapter, but it's solidified and maintained by mastering a tool that might surprise you: words.

Words resonate on a cellular level—and I mean that literally. Our bodies internalize what we say, both positively and negatively. Words create our reality. They shape it, expand it, or limit it. They help us build spiritual muscle or they distract us from what needs to be done. They lead us into new experiences or they ensure that we will repeat the old ones. They are how we translate what we feel into something other people can understand. So if we want clarity that matters and lasts, one of the best tools at our disposal is our words.

My 2013 commitment list provides the perfect examples. When I wrote those words down, they took on new meaning. They reflected what I thought and what

I believed. By writing them down, I forged an informal contract with myself. They helped me clarify my values, and someday those values will be shared with someone who will equally hold me accountable to them.

It's not just in what we write. Our spoken words also have power. So after going through my experience at the Bentley and then dedicating myself to building spiritual muscle, I also decided to start speaking about my transformation to see if I could have an impact on other people's lives—this time for the better.

When I began using words to show my vulnerability to others, the unexpected happened. People began opening up and becoming vulnerable with me—not just people who were already close to me, but also people I never would have expected to share anything personal about their lives. These conversations had, and continue to have, a positive impact on me. Every time someone else's life has been positively affected by my story, I, too, grow and have more joy in my own life.

TO IMPROVE MY SKILLS WITH WORDS, I tried a little experiment that you might want to repeat. For the sixteen or so hours you're awake during the day, force yourself to say only positive things, whether they're affirmations of yourself or other people. Then see how you feel at the end of the day. I predict you'll find the impact is astonishing. When I did this, I found that my words gave clarity to my feelings, and those feelings were the starting point for my transformation. I discovered that my words could actually change my feelings and my actions that stemmed from those feelings.

Our personal stories are always playing inside our heads. Those words affect how we see ourselves and how we show up in the world. Because we have the power to change the words flowing through us, we can change the experiences of our lives. Simply put, our perspective is a choice. Many times we have no control over things that can happen to us in life, only our reaction to those events or circumstances. Words are different, because we can control what we say.

Words begin the process of helping us realize what's missing. They are verbal triggers for change. For instance, by December 2011, I had allowed myself to become numb. Even though I'd had that transformative moment a month earlier, I had slowly forgotten how incredible it feels to be filled with joy because I wasn't actively recognizing the things that brought me joy. I literally couldn't get myself to feel a spark inside of me. In early February 2012, Stephen McGhee finally got through to me.

We were sitting in my office and Stephen asked me to describe what I felt the most exciting trip of my life would look like. I replied that it would be a father-and-son helicopter trip around the world, where my son and I would explore new cultures, hike, fish, and sit around the campfire each night reading the Bible together without any electronic media in sight. When I finished describing this perfect adventure to Stephen, I had the biggest smile on my face. It felt incredible.

It wasn't easy, but in time I began to literally feel again. I used my vision and my words to gain clarity around how I was fighting for joy. I had nothing to lose, and if I didn't make positive declarations, I was doomed.

When words bring clarity, they have the power to drive out the fear that cripples us. When taken to an extreme, fear can control our choices and, therefore, our lives. Fear is actually born out of a need for control.

As a child, my mother wasn't really "there" even when she was there, and I often was put in the position of feeling like I had to look after my dad throughout my teen years and into my twenties. Family never represented a safe harbor for me the way it does for many people, and I felt alone in the world. When things went wrong, there were no parents for me to run to who would make me feel that sense of security. The more out of control I feel in situations, like flying or being in a hotel room alone, the more anxious I become because I feel isolated and without a deeply embedded sense of security.

But I am growing in this area. One way I combat the fear that arises from not being in control is by using words creatively to connect language with my imagination and telling a new story. For example, when I board an airplane and put on my seat belt, I imagine myself walking through the Denver airport at the end of the trip. I describe to myself what it looks and feels like for me to be back home with my feet walking down the concourse, the weight of my bag on my right shoulder and my briefcase in my left hand, the feeling of the wind coming through my hair as the airport doors open and I see the sun shining on the Rocky Mountains. I use my words to create an alternative experience, and the fear gets managed by seeing the outcome I want.

The same things apply to our vision as leaders: We have to let ourselves imagine what things are going to look like when everything is done and the mission has been successfully accomplished. There's something incredible about using a part of us that really doesn't know any boundaries. We see ourselves on the other side of an experience and we stop focusing on the difficulties we have to go through to get there. We know it will be a rough journey from Point A to Point B, but we use words to focus only on Point B.

We all have thoughts that we find hard to believe would ever go through our heads. In the grips of depression, we might fear that we would someday act on such thoughts. This can take us a step closer to that point of wondering if the world—especially those we love—would be better without us in it. This is the message of fear and chaos, not clarity. It is a bitter lie. Clarity helps us take a step back and moves us to a better place.

One way I get to that better place is by saying a single, simple word: "Next." When thoughts are coming into my mind that I don't like, I consciously speak to them with a hint of laughter in my tone: "Next." I say it out loud and I enunciate. And it works. I just say "Next" and let the next thought in (kicking out the offending one in the process). The gentle laughter in my tone is me refusing to give some random thought any credibility of being rational or worthy of my time. Scripture calls this taking every thought captive.

If a thought is particularly unsettling and this doesn't work, I take myself back to a time when I was in immense pain and once again use imagination to address the cause of the troubles, instead of just looking at or feeling the effect.

Words create healing experiences.

One parting thought about the words we choose: Words can expand or contract our abilities, including how effective we are with the time we've been given. Committing to the things in life we want to accomplish only takes us halfway. Going the distance requires that we recommit daily, through words, to the life we want to create. Being clear in our language—to ourselves and others—about what we want in life is critical. This allows us to set limits on how we spend and invest our time.

Those limits require the discipline of being able to say "no." It took a long time for me to realize that saying "no" takes more of a commitment (and recommitment) than saying "yes." A friend of mine once told me that "'no' is a one-word complete sentence with tremendous power." This wisdom has served me well. When we say "no," we are being clear about our values and our boundaries. We can use one perfect word with a perfectly clear meaning, and we don't have to justify anything else about our actions.

VINCE LOMBARDI, the legendary Green Bay Packers football coach, used to say, "Discipline isn't something that you do to someone; it's something you do for them."

That's a perfect example of an authority expressing his value (discipline) in a clear and understandable way. And he lived that value in equally clear and understandable ways. Through his words and his actions, Lombardi said, "I'm not doing this to hurt you, so don't act like a victim. I'm doing this to make you a better football player and a better person off the field." His words and his actions gave clarity to his belief in discipline.

That type of clarity is hard to come by.

The clearer we are about our values, however, the more distinctive we are in our language, in our actions, and in how we spend our time. When we're clear, the right words find us and the right actions flow from us.

In fact, the clearer we become, the fewer words we actually need. We can use fewer words because we're not trying to serve multiple masters or force our message. My greatest teachers in life didn't use force. They conveyed their values through a few words, many actions, and much silence.

I tend to gravitate toward people in the "back nine holes" of their lives because they tend to be so clear in who they are and have learned invaluable life wisdom. They tend to dispense that wisdom in very understandable and sometimes very cutting ways. They don't give you the watered-down version or the shades of gray; they give you what you need.

ANOTHER IMPORTANT ASPECT of clarity involves the influences we allow into our lives, and that includes the media we consume. I've become very clear on what aspects of the culture I will and will not consume. If the entertainment or news media are promoting values I don't agree with, I don't participate. You've probably heard the expression, "You are what you eat." Well, you also are what you listen to and watch. If you are "eating" a lot of media with values you don't have, guess what happens? The media changes you.

The words and actions we hear and see in media can become ours if we're not careful. I've seen that happen with children, where they begin to adopt the words (and values) they've heard on TV or in video games. So be very clear about your filters and how they're working, and don't be afraid to vote with your dollars on what content you're willing to let into your mind.

It's just as important, of course, to be clear about the people we let into our lives. As my mother used to tell me, it's much easier for bad people to pull us down than for good people to pull us up.

In 2013, I got very clear on the difference between acquaintances and friends. I had learned how critical it was to be vigilant about the people you surround yourself with. Motivational speaker Jim Rohn said, "You are the average of the five people you spend the most time with." I agree. When you're around people who are in alignment and you share similar values, you all grow stronger because of it. The writer of Proverbs put it this way: "As iron sharpens iron, so one person sharpens another" (Proverbs 27:17). When I think back to times in my life when I wasn't living in alignment, it's clear I had surrounded myself with people who valued the wrong things and it more than rubbed off on me, though I didn't fully realize it at the time.

Because of my insecurities, I assumed that most of the nice things people did for me while I was married were tied to the family I'd married into. I then assumed those people thought less of me after my divorce. Worse, I felt like I had let some of those people down or embarrassed them. As I developed spiritual muscle, I learned to proactively seek clarity about what other people think of me rather than just living with my assumptions.

I actually learned this lesson thanks to my favorite barber in Denver. I was in doubt about a person I deeply respected, and whom I believed did not like me because of my divorce. The man was a successful business leader who, much like my father-in-law, had invested in me personally and professionally. My barber gave me some incredible advice. He asked me to stop second-guessing this man's behavior and actually take the time to reach out and find out for myself how he really felt. He encouraged me to meet with him to try and separate fact from fiction.

I followed his advice and when we met, I was surprised at how completely off base I truly was regarding his opinion of me. To this day, he remains supportive of me and checks in with me on how things are going in my new life.

Clarity. It's a powerful thing.

CLARITY IS ALSO THE GATEWAY to finding joy in the little things in life. Clarity allows us to be immediately grateful for all the blessings and to learn even more from our failures.

One of the reasons I've done things like write the commitment list I mentioned earlier is because I need to clarify my vision for a family going forward. Libby and I lacked this clarity in our marriage, and our family suffered because of it. Now my clarity gives me the confidence that I will continue to create a safe harbor for my son, whether my son and I create a new family or not.

At some point we all have to trust our decisions, our leadership, our business, and the pilot of the plane (when we fear flying). We have to let go and just "be."

Chapter 16

# Don't "Should" on Yourself

"We gather our arms full of guilt as
though it were precious stuff. It must be
that we want it that way."

—John Steinbeck

CHANGED SCHOOLS GROWING UP more often than most
kids changed socks.

By the time I reached the sixth grade, I had enrolled in
my fifth school. I moved to a new school midway through
the eighth grade, and I stayed in that district through high
school—four and half years with the same classmates. It
brought some stability, yet I still struggled to feel like I
fit in.

It was junior high school, that time in life when almost
everyone feels like a misfit—budding teenagers trying to
figure out how we fit into the world when our bodies,
intellect, social skills, emotions, maturity, and wisdom
all seem to be racing forward at different speeds and on
different tracks.

It didn't help that I already was well on my way
to living with a victim mentality and struggling with

self-confidence and self-esteem. So when I arrived at Creighton Junior High, I immediately ran into cliques that had been formed from childhood sports teams and from the students' elementary school years together. I never penetrated those groups, and I developed feelings of rejection because I wasn't embraced by many of those kids, even though they, too, were probably struggling with their own issues of self-confidence and self-esteem.

So before going to my ten-year high school reunion in 1997, I convinced myself that it would be difficult to see the people I remembered treating me so poorly. I debated whether to just stay home, but ultimately I decided to show up, even if it meant seeing some of the people who would make me uncomfortable and bring back painful memories. I decided I would take the offensive and confront those I saw as my tormentors. I thought I was being brave, but I still had a lot to learn about courage.

When I arrived at the reunion, a guy approached me and pulled me aside almost as soon as I entered the front door. We exchanged small talk for about two minutes before I realized he had another agenda. He had been waiting a long time to clear his heart, so as the chitchat came to a close, he paused for a second and then fired the question he'd been carrying with him for more than a decade: "Do you realize the damage you did to me back in high school because you wouldn't accept me?"

I was stunned. I had been so focused on all the harm people had caused me that I had no idea this man had spent years carrying the baggage of how I'd hurt him. As he spoke, I wasn't sure what I had done to make him feel that way, but I later recalled the teasing that had gone on in our physics class and that one time I'd embarrassed him in front of the other students. I suspect he came to the reunion to confront me (and maybe others) on the advice of a counselor. I apologized and we parted ways, not as friends but certainly not as enemies.

You might think I would have learned something from his courage and his approach, but I missed a golden opportunity to redirect my own course that evening. Instead, I immediately turned to my agenda of confronting people in a far less healthy way. I had a major ax to grind with a few people, and I went about grinding it.

At the reunion I sought out one of the kids who had bullied me. I made a point of belittling him in front of others there because he was selling used cars, while I was selling for a high-tech company. And I made a snarky comment about "career choices" to a girl who had posed for a men's magazine. I was out for blood, and I got it. I literally targeted a handful of people to make them feel how I did when we were teenagers (very mature of me, I know).

I ended up drinking too much and figuratively crying on the shoulder of an old friend, giving her my sob story about how poorly I'd been treated.

As I look back on that night, I'm appalled by my behavior. It stands out in stark contrast to the classmate who confronted me with the purpose of healing, not the purpose of retribution. It took a lot of strength for him to tell me what was in his heart and to show that he was trying to leave his past behind and embrace his future. He didn't worry about what he should or shouldn't say about things that had happened so many years before. He knew he could never truly let this conflict go until he'd taken a step of action in a positive way. Who knows, maybe he even forgave me that night as part of his own process of moving on to better things. I hope so.

For years, I lacked the courage to act on that type of conviction—to do what my heart was telling me to do rather than what I thought everyone else wanted or expected me to do, or what my wounded pride was telling me to do. And even after this man showed me an example of the courage I needed, I continued to "should" all over myself.

I'M NOT SURE where I first heard the phrase "don't 'should' on yourself," but as far as I can tell it was coined by Clayton Barbeau, a psychologist in California. When we tell ourselves that we have an obligation to do something because other people tell us we "should" or because we think we "should" so we can please other people, then we're "shoulding" ourselves.

This cognitive distortion sets us up for trouble, even when our "shoulds" are good. The world tells us what we should do—you *should* lose weight, you *should* volunteer at the homeless shelter, you *should* read more books, you *should* exercise more regularly, you *should* save money, you *should* settle down with a specific type of person—and it all sounds good, because it is good. But if we're doing all these good things for all the wrong reasons—to please other people, to atone for our mistakes, to hide from our weaknesses—then all the good is meaningless. Worse than that, it can further damage our core.

When we live based on what we think we "should" do, we lose sight of what we want or need—which is often very different from what we think we "should" do. It also means that we turn into the person we're "supposed" to be rather than the person we are meant to be—the person we really *are*. And when we aren't who we really are, the joy gets sucked right out of our lives. We're pretenders. Posers. Fakes. Phonies. And we end up surrounding ourselves with other pretenders, fakes, and phonies.

Instead of valuing ourselves simply for who we are, we end up tying our value to the things we do or the people we want to please. We've given up our power and we're letting them decide what amount of value we really provide—a double whammy.

The classmate at my reunion wasn't living for anyone else. He wasn't worried about my opinion of him. The world might have told him to keep his mouth shut and forget it, or to fight back and get "even" with his tormentors (like I tried to), but surely it was his heart that told him to take a different approach, one that brought healing: Move away from being a victim by talking honestly about how he had felt all those years ago. Even if a professional gave him advice, nobody knew what was best for him except for him. And nobody could take his steps for him. He had to do it himself. And he did.

THE MOMENT WE DECLARE that we're no longer a victim and that we're not going to spend our lives trying to fulfill what we imagine are the expectations of others, we've taken a huge step forward. The moment we shift our focus away from what we think we're lacking to what we can create next, the new creations start to unfold. The moment we decide to stop "shoulding" on ourselves, the good (and the great) begin to happen.

Every journey starts with a single step that carries us away from the past, so we have to consciously choose the direction in which we want to go. With each new step, the scenery changes and becomes quite different from where we began. Once we make that commitment, our perspective will usually shift, and we start to see things we literally couldn't see before—things (and people) that were there the whole time.

I saw this play out in my life not long after I stopped "shoulding" on myself and started following my heart wisdom. I was asked to give a speech to a group of nearly seventy CEOs about overcoming the biggest obstacle in my career. Instead of sharing the typical business-failure story, I decided to hit the "play" button on vulnerability and share with them the biggest obstacle I had to overcome as a man: how I had lost my way by seeking validation from the world and trying to please others rather than by staying true to myself.

Something inside me was telling me that even if I could reach just one person, it would be worth the fear I felt from sharing my story with a group of powerful men and women. I shared this with the audience about one minute into the speech, saying, "The message I am going to deliver today is hopefully for the benefit of everyone attending the conference, but I am specifically delivering my message to one person who I believe is currently experiencing a very tough period in their life." Before leaving the stage, I ended my talk by telling the audience that if I had reached that "one person" tonight, I would remain open to him or her 24/7 for as long as I was needed.

About four days later, one of the CEOs in the audience called and introduced himself.

"I want to spend some time with you," he said. "I was the person you were giving your speech to last week."

We met for breakfast, and he told me how he had jumped into the parade for all the wrong reasons. He was the leader of a multimillion-dollar company and had done extremely well in the business world, but he needed help.

"Everybody thinks I'm great on the outside," he said, "but on the inside, I'm in a lot of pain."

He couldn't find peace and was restless all the time. He was unable to sleep, full of worry, and his wife was growing more and more concerned about him. He was surrounded by the "shoulds" and the expectations that he believed were coming from those around him. He didn't know how to break out of this cycle, and he knew from my speech that I'd gone through a similar difficult process.

He was right.

I described for him many of the experiences and tools I've laid out in this book. It starts with confronting the past in a meaningful and organized way. I described the need to take action driven by long-term conscious design, rather than just reacting to fleeting feelings. I talked about rediscovering the people and things in life that bring him joy, and about the need to commit, and recommit, to serving a larger purpose outside of himself and his business. That purpose may include making money, but that's only one part of the goal. The larger intention is to serve from a place of helping everyone, not just yourself.

"If I hadn't turned myself over to God," I told him that morning, "I would have just re-created the same situation that caused my problems in the first place. Isn't it funny how the feeling of anxiety goes away after you confront yourself in a productive way and begin serving others?"

Naturally, he was filled with doubts.

"I don't think I have the capacity to serve others anymore," he said.

"You still have that capacity," I said, "but your cup is empty because you've been focused on appeasing others. You haven't been true to yourself."

"I just want to be happy," he told me.

"Happiness doesn't exist inside of you," I reminded him. "Joy lives there, but happiness doesn't."

My new friend was "shoulding" on himself. He felt trapped because of what he perceived were all the expectations of him from his wife, children, parents, friends, other CEOs, and so on. He was literally living to keep them happy and accepting of what he was doing. His "shoulding" wouldn't allow him to make life choices that might yield a new career path and a lower income level.

How many times do we hear that from people? They take the big promotion, maybe move to a different city, only to discover how lonely it is and how deeply they miss their old life. "Shoulding" is usually the reason for their emptiness because they are pursuing something that they perceive others want or need them to do.

The CEO and I met and emailed several times during the next few months, and those conversations were a big step in a new direction for him, but they also were another step in the process of my own transformation. While I feel confident I helped him, I'm even more positive that he helped *me* move forward because he showed me what I could accomplish in terms of my own work. I'm a better person now because of him.

While I felt blessed to have a meaningful impact on his life, I also knew it wouldn't stop with him.

When I began my speech, I was specifically focused on helping one person, and this is what happened. However, I predict he will continue to have a positive impact on the hundreds of people who work for him and in the other circles he's a part of. Those people will then go on to have an impact on others.

We are all connected.

APPEASEMENT is one of the most difficult tendencies to avoid in life, because we so often want to be liked by others and not to rock the boat. We don't want to disappoint our boss, so we accept a position we really don't want. We don't want to say anything when someone we want to please plans a social event with people we want nothing to do with.

Rather than being clear by setting boundaries about our values, we indirectly give people permission to violate those values. We appease with the word "yes" instead of standing strong by saying "no." That's why it's important to have friends and, most importantly, a spouse who share your values. When you are equally yoked, so to speak, to your values, you can live in alignment with each other rather than trying to appease each other.

When our values aren't aligned with the people we're involved with each day, we have to decide if we are going to say something or just go along. It can be so much easier, or so we think, to avoid speaking up and hope that something we really need to confront will magically go away. Nothing standing in the way of our growth as a human being, however, goes away on its own. We must deal with it, or it will only come back in some larger and more painful form.

You may have heard the expression "Let go, and let God." It means that we are called to do our part in the world but that God is in control of the results. There are times when God calls us to step in and take action, but the results of those actions ultimately are out of our control or influence. And, frankly, that's a good thing. Most of us have been in a relationship and wanted an outcome that didn't come to pass. We didn't understand it at the time, but later in life we came to realize the blessing of that unanswered prayer.

I ONCE HEARD SOMEONE on the radio say that he'd gotten his "PhD in pain." It made me laugh. His message was about having to rebuild his life without a road map. In the past few years I've tried to build a map that I can share with others who are living in what I imagine is similar to the pain I was once feeling.

I want to stop the cycle of "shoulding" and victimization. The only way to do this is through practicing the discipline of knowing ourselves in the deepest possible ways—knowing our strengths and our weaknesses, knowing our darkness and our light—and then going after what we want, not what we think we *should* want.

Chapter 17

# The Creative Power of Focus

"If a man does not know to what port he
is steering, no wind is favorable to him."

—*Seneca*

WAS FOURTEEN YEARS OLD when I earned the honor
of serving as senior patrol leader in the Boy Scouts—a
very big deal for me because my peers voted me into the
position.

At one of our meetings, however, I got into an argument with our scoutmaster, Tom, and things became
heated. I took a disagreement and turned it into a power
struggle that I had no chance of winning. I challenged
him in front of the whole troop, and when I didn't get my
way, I walked to the back where the rest of the troop was
sitting, took out my pocketknife, cut off my senior patrol
leader patch, and handed it to him.

*I'm the senior patrol leader,* I thought defiantly, *and I've
got as much say in the process as you do.*

In circumstances like these, I was certain I was the
victim. And in this case, I was equally sure that Tom
would see that he was wrong and that he was treating me

unfairly. As soon as he recognized the error of his ways, I'd get my patch back and we could all move forward with our lives. He didn't back down, however, and I left that night without my patch or my coveted role in the troop.

A few nights later, Tom and his assistant scoutmaster, Hank, came to my house to discuss the situation. I was living with my mother at the time, but my dad came over for the meeting. I sat crying over what had happened as Tom explained what I'd done and why I was wrong to cut off my patch. He made things very clear that my behavior wasn't appropriate or respectful to him or my peers—that wasn't the way things worked, in Scouting or in life. He let all of us know that getting my position back within the Scouts wasn't going to be easy, but that this experience could be a good teacher to me for future character development and how I planned to show up in the world.

A full six months passed before I earned back the role of senior patrol leader, but it felt even longer because the Boy Scouts were a major part of my life. It was a powerful lesson in humility and in getting what we focus on: When we focus on being a victim, we end up living as one.

My scoutmaster could have said, "Tim, stop being a victim. I'm taking your senior patrol badge and this conversation is over." Instead, he went the extra step by taking the time to come to my house to meet with my parents and me, and trying to do something to help me see how my actions had resulted in this consequence. It took a lot of thought and effort on his part, and he showed what a true leader was; he cared enough about his entire troop to close the loop on the conflict. Thirty years later, I'm still thinking about the effect this had on me.

It took me a long time, however, to fully learn Tom's lesson about how seeing yourself as a victim never serves you well. Indeed, it wasn't until after my experience at the Bentley that I really "got it" in a way that I could "live it" more fully.

Does that ever happen to you? I'm guessing it does. Most of us learn lessons in an intellectual way and maybe even make some effort to change, but ultimately slide back into our old and comfortable habits because we never fully embraced the lesson at a deeper, heart-wisdom level. Until we make that connection, we can't really transform our lives.

After my experience in New York, I made a promise to God that if I came out safely on the other side of the crisis, I'd never allow myself to use the victim mind-set again.

Lately, it's come to me that God has His own way of enforcing this agreement. If I start to slide back or focus on being a victim, I have an immediate and negative physiological response within my body. If I begin to feel or act selfishly, I quickly experience anxiety and discomfort. The more victimized I feel, the more intensely negative my feelings. My wiring is different now because I wasn't the only one who kept his agreement in these circumstances—so did God.

We become victims by making a step-by-step commitment to that belief system. We become victorious in exactly the same way: making a commitment to a belief system that supports victory. It's all a matter of what we focus on.

REGARDLESS OF WHAT WE TRY TO ACCOMPLISH, some people on the sidelines will tell us not to do it—don't take the risk, the market will never accept your ideas, it's over-saturated with competitors, and your plans are just plain crazy. The same holds true with human relationships, especially when we're trying to repair a relationship that's been severely damaged. I've pretty much come to believe that when the naysayers are at their loudest, I know I'm on the right track. Where we see opportunities, our critics only see problems and are usually quick to dispense their negative words.

As I mentioned earlier, we must choose carefully the words we pay attention to—the words we use and the words we listen to when others speak to or about us. What we focus on is what we will create, whether that creation is the same fear and pain we've known for years (or a higher level of it) or something entirely new.

WHEN WE LOSE FOCUS on the right things, we put ourselves in the crosshairs of temptation. I used to think temptation was just being tempted by something I didn't or couldn't have, but temptations are far broader than that. For instance, there are countless temptations to become a victim inside our own mind. There are temptations to revert to childhood and take the easy route (or possibly the familiar route) and blame others for what we think or feel.

One critical tool for resisting temptation is developing the discipline to set clear boundaries and being vigilant about protecting them. Boundaries protect us from temptations and from being vulnerable when we don't need to be. We need very clear boundaries within ourselves, along with the confidence to be able to tell what those boundaries are. This will create clarity, and clarity creates peace.

As a leader, I know that the greater my integrity, the higher I will perform. The greater my integrity, the higher the level of trust I'll get from the people I'm leading and the higher they will perform. As leaders, our values, whether we know it or not, empower others as they watch, absorb, and learn from us. Our family watches how we lead at work, our coworkers watch how we lead at home and in the community, and our friends watch how we lead our families and how we lead in business. Our personal values are integrated into everything we do: the way we lead in business, the way we lead our families, the way we lead in our community. It is called life leadership, and it is the most powerful type of leading I know.

SINCE I BEGAN BUILDING SPIRITUAL MUSCLE, I've kept my focus on being as humble as possible. As my humility has grown, my world has expanded exponentially, and through a consistent focus on my core values, I've also gained self-esteem.

In business, when we focus on humility and surround ourselves with people who are smarter than us that we can delegate responsibility to, we are putting control into the hands of the right people.

A lack of humility, on the other hand, can lead to disaster. People lose respect for arrogant leaders. If they follow those leaders, it's for the wrong reasons, and the trust is easily broken when times get tough. A lack of humility also shows up in stubbornness and pride that prevent us from correcting our course sooner rather than later. For instance, I needed to check my ego far sooner than I did when I was running the Denver radio stations. Instead, I was blinded by my pride, so I couldn't see that the stations weren't going to make it. In life I'm reminded of the immense wisdom that comes when we seek answers differently because we know that we don't know. I've been on the receiving end of people who take a bad situation and make it worse because they don't know that they don't know. Their ego keeps getting in the way, so they believe opinion and facts are the same thing. The reality, as former U.S. senator Daniel Patrick Moynihan put it, is that we can have our own opinions, but we can't have our own facts. Humility will always show us the difference.

AS WE MOVE TOWARD LIVING INTO ALIGNMENT, it's helpful to be reminded about where we came from in order to see how much progress we've made. It's important to celebrate little victories and honor our own growth. Mastery doesn't happen overnight, so we need to extend grace and compassion to ourselves.

Chapter 18

# Building a Trust Fund

"The best executive is one who has
sense enough to pick good people
to do what he wants done, and self-
restraint enough to keep from meddling
with them while they do it."

*—Theodore Roosevelt*

A T THE AGE OF SIXTEEN, after saving for two years
working at McDonald's and installing carpet with
my father, I bought my first car—a Volkswagen Rabbit.
It wasn't the basic Rabbit, but a souped-up version with
the faster engine.

You know what a car represents to any sixteen-year-
old: freedom.

For me, that freedom was multiplied by my desire to
escape my past. But my much-desired freedom didn't last.

Fifty-eight days after I turned sixteen, I ran a red light
as another driver was turning left. There were no serious
injuries in the crash, at least not to the people involved.
The Rabbit, on the other hand, went to junkyard heaven.

I was living with my mother, who by this time had begun to turn her life around with the help of Alcoholics Anonymous. She had two cars, one that she drove and one that she was trying to sell. So I figured I could drive one of those until I saved up enough for another car of my own. My mother, however, saw things differently. She didn't trust me to drive her car and she knew I needed to learn about living with the consequences of my actions, so she wouldn't allow me to drive either of her cars. (Nationwide Insurance seemed to support her opinion by doubling my rate.)

As you might guess, this left me both upset at my mom and stranded at home. I had no way to go see my girlfriend, who lived about eight miles away, and there was no bus service to my school. We had moved out of neighborhoods served in my high school's district, and I was six miles from the school I was attending. So to get to school I had to ride the 1981 red Pugh moped I had bought when I was thirteen.

Despite the few times I had dropped the moped on the pavement due to hitting sand on the road, it still ran marginally well. Showing up to my high school on a moped instead of my car was another matter entirely when it came to the ridicule I received from other students in my class. The heckling served as another reminder of the mistake I had made in wrecking my car. I was determined to figure out another solution to my transportation dilemma.

One night while my mom was sleeping, I sneaked out of the house and made a copy of the key to her Audi. The next time she went to her AA meeting, I took the car to see my girlfriend. This went on for about three weeks, including a few times that I waited for my mother to leave for work and took her car to school. My plan by all appearances seemed to be working flawlessly until the night I drove home from seeing my girlfriend and saw her other vehicle parked in the carport.

It was bad enough that she was waiting for me to return, but I found a way to make things even worse. I couldn't face her and what she'd say to me, so I decided not to go home. Instead, I temporarily moved in with some older friends who had graduated high school two years earlier and who lived on their own. I was somehow thinking this would magically solve the problem. For the next few days, I went to school in the Audi, didn't call my mom, and hid from her like a coward.

One Friday morning I woke up to find that the Audi was gone. My mother had figured out where I was, and she had "repossessed" her car in the middle of a very cold February night. I now had to walk to school in the bitter cold from my older friends' house, as none of them could get motivated from their hangovers to give me a ride to school.

At that point she knew I had to come home, and I knew it, too. When I walked into our small apartment, my mom was still at work, but I found a one-page letter from her on our table. In the letter, she expressed her disappointment in my character and told me I was untrustworthy and that she couldn't believe what I'd done. When she finally arrived home that night, she didn't say a word to me for over an hour. It was the most deafening silence I'd ever heard.

I still remember the emotional response that came with reading her letter. You never forget those moments when you break someone's trust, especially when it's someone you care about deeply. It left a permanent mark on me, and I kept that letter for many years. Decades later, it still hurts to think about it.

While her letter crushed me at the time, it didn't do anything to keep me from feeling like a victim instead of a participant in the events that had happened with the car. I wasn't ready to deal with the consequences of my actions. So instead of owning up to my mistakes and working through issues I had created with my mother, I left her home less than one month later and moved in with my dad.

I was untrustworthy, and I was unwilling to own what I had done. Instead, I ran from it and traded in a good living situation for a very difficult one. It took me eight months to confront the problem and talk honestly with my mother. When we finally reconciled, she told me a proverb about a block of wood. Every time you drill holes in the wood, she said, the stability of the wood deteriorates. You can put putty over the drilled holes and sand it down so it looks as if the holes don't exist, but they're always there, with each hole making the wood weaker.

It would take a long time to repair the damage I'd done to our relationship, and, frankly, the holes in that block of wood never fully went away. My mother could forgive me, which she did, but it probably took seven years for her to move from a "trust but verify" mind-set to one of unconditional trust, and I suspect she always wondered if I'd betray her trust again.

The entire incident reminds me of a riddle: "What takes a lifetime to build and only a moment to lose?"

Trust, of course.

WE BUILD TRUST OVER TIME, and it becomes the cornerstone of all relationships—spiritually, personally, and professionally. It is earned by the way we live out our commitment to our core values and the character we display through our daily actions.

I've discovered the hard way that this begins with trusting myself. Trusting ourselves makes it easier for others to trust us. And we learn to trust ourselves by learning to trust our experiences. Bad experiences, though difficult at the time, help shape us for a larger purpose. We discover that our characters can be positively affected by even the most negative of events.

If we decide to enter any type of relationship without trust as the foundation of our moral code and our behavior, then we can forget about developing long-term relationships. Without trust, we'll end up burning through jobs, friendships, spouses, and colleagues.

Unfortunately, too many businesspeople tie their ethical decisions to dollar amounts. They justify indiscretions by saying the actions didn't involve "much" money and lie to themselves by saying they wouldn't do something "wrong" if it involved "a lot" of money. Conveniently, their definition of "a lot" always adjusts to higher and higher amounts.

The things I've learned to trust above all others now revolve around faith, family, and friends. We never get anywhere in life based solely on our own efforts. Everything from the smallest atomic particle to the largest event in the universe is a co-creation. We need other people and we need God.

If we love what we do for a living and commit to it for the long term, we're going to help ourselves as well as many others around us. Likewise, if we don't trust in ourselves, our products, or our company, then our clients and customers will sense that lack of faith and they won't trust us, either. They pick up on this regardless of how well we attempt to disguise it. The same holds true with our families.

ONE OF THE WAYS we develop trustworthiness growing up is through organized sports. It puts us in situations where we must learn to trust ourselves, trust others, and earn the trust of our peers. We learn to trust adult coaches and to get along with the other teammates, and we begin to learn who we are and what values we'll embrace.

Like anything else, however, athletics can take us places we don't need to go. For me, this happened when competitive triathlons became a way for me to isolate myself from my problems and the very people who might help me the most. I placed my trust in the wrong things: my athletic abilities, the adrenaline rush, the chance to use training as a distraction, finding self-worth in how well I competed, using workouts as an excuse to avoid the things I needed to confront.

In March 2008, I started participating in Half IRON-MAN triathlon competitions. That's 1.2 miles of swimming, a 56-mile bike ride, and a 13.1-mile run, all done consecutively for a total of 70.3 miles.

I successfully completed three Half IRONMAN events in Oceanside, California; Lawrence, Kansas; and Austin, Texas. Then I decided to attempt something more—a full IRONMAN. So, as the Denver radio stations were starting to fail, I began training for the Arizona IRONMAN—a 2.4-mile swim, a 112-mile bike ride, and a 26.2-mile run, for a total of 140.6 miles.

I felt the training was allowing me to clear my head in order to be a better leader. I was able to work "on" the business instead of just "in" the business because of my intense focus and thinking over the long distances of swimming, biking, and running. However, the real running I was doing was from the decision I needed to make about what to do with the Denver radio stations in September 2008, when we were seeing more signs about the economy turning and the stations not being able to support themselves financially.

In retrospect, shutting down the stations in the autumn of 2008 would have been a better decision than waiting until June 2009 to put the stations on autopilot. We left them with a skeleton staff of two people while we waited for the FCC to approve the sale and for the buyer to transfer funds and take full control, which finally happened in February 2010.

With my self-esteem tied to radio, I began to look for a new outlet to provide me with an identity that wasn't associated with being a failure. I quickly tied my sense of worth to becoming an IRONMAN and having that "140.6" sticker on the back of my car as I trained. I thought accomplishing that feat would build up my self-esteem.

Instead, it only made matters worse. I planned on competing in two or three IRONMAN events a year, and I was training nearly thirty hours per week. That only added to the strains on my marriage. I was self-absorbed, and I found ways to justify my pursuits and vilify my wife's lack of understanding and support. *If she can't deal with an IRONMAN as a husband*, I thought, *then she'll have to find a new husband*. It's hard for me to look back now and acknowledge that this selfish thought actually went through my head. The irony here of her not understanding is that she made an effort to go on many of my longer bicycle training rides (sixty-plus miles) so we could be together.

The day before my first full IRONMAN, Libby and I got into a heated argument about the time I was spending on training and how obsessed I had become with what I would, or wouldn't, eat or drink. I think she was also fatigued by constantly hearing about triathlons and the culture and community I was trying to plug myself into. That only served to increase the angst and pressure I felt from life.

The Arizona IRONMAN started at 6 A.M., and it was still dark out and chilly that November morning. The competition began with the swimming leg, so I jumped into the super-cold water with two thousand other swimmers.

Unlike the Half IRONMAN competitions I'd done, where the swimming had begun in staggered age-group waves, the longer race in Arizona began with everyone crammed together in the water underneath several bridge pillars. People thrashed around, inadvertently hitting one another. Despite all the training I'd done for the event, I instantly sensed that I was out of my element. I felt unsafe in water this cold and competing with this many people. I trusted my swimming abilities; I had been exposed to open water and swimming pools since I was a baby in Florida, and I had once helped save a man from drowning off the coast of Manly Beach in Australia. But on this day, I was overcome by a fear of being vulnerable in open water with poor visibility and people hitting me from seemingly all angles. I didn't feel in control.

I swam for almost 1.2 miles—half the distance—before I had what my doctor later told me was a "vasovagal response." My blood pressure had dropped significantly, and I essentially blacked out after feeling chest pains and intense light-headedness. Fortunately, I was close enough to the shoreline to realize I was losing consciousness, and

I swam toward it until a man working in the race pulled me out of the water.

I quit the race and had to take the "Walk of Shame" as a not-so-proud owner of a DNF stamp—"Did Not Finish." I was equally embarrassed to have someone from the race's medical staff perform a health checkup on me. Obviously, this wasn't what I was expecting, nor was it something I wanted to explain to all my friends who were anxious to hear of my success from the race. With my wetsuit unzipped, I walked away from the race while everybody else went on with the triathlon.

*Seventeen months of regimented physical training and regimented eating just went down the tubes,* I thought.

According to my doctor, a vasovagal response can be a lifesaving fight-or-flight mechanism where the body shuts down when your blood pressure gets too high. If your body senses that you're going to have a heart attack, it can suddenly drop your blood pressure as a safety valve.

I was told that my response happened purely for physical reasons, but now I think it was a mixture of mental and emotional anxiety. I had built a false god by believing and wrongly trusting that being an IRON-MAN was one of the most important things in life. In retrospect, I've come to the conclusion that losing consciousness in the water was triggered because I could no longer take the pressure I'd been putting on myself. I had made all these false demands of myself, and they caught up with me in the water when my body imploded. My identity and self-worth had been chained to this race, and only later, when I reframed it, did I realize how ridiculous that was.

I think this was my first anxiety attack, and it was driven by my own expectations. Ironically, this type of intense anxiety ultimately foreshadowed what happened three years later at the Bentley Hotel in New York.

At the time, however, my failure to finish the race simply became one more strike against my self-esteem, one more failure, one more reason to push even harder in life to prove myself. I'd been so successful in so much of my life, but now I had failed as an IRONMAN, my radio business was floundering, and my marriage was in the beginning stages of breaking down. Trying to atone for these failures is what led me to push myself so hard when I was running Sign Language, which only added to my anxieties.

THERE ARE SEVERAL WAYS I've learned to develop trust as a spiritual muscle in recent years.

The first is when I'm getting to know someone, personally or professionally, and we encounter that first test that comes with inevitable relational friction. I call a quick time-out; I stop everything and ask, "What do you need? What is it that you want right now?" As long as it doesn't violate my values, I try to provide that need for the other person.

This is an incredible bridge-builder because the moment is all about serving the other person and our relationship. This usually generates an immediate and positive reaction from the other person because an act of service does more to build or rebuild trust than just about anything else. It can take the relationship to the next level.

This is one way of jumping into the parade. You're not leading the other person; you're leading the relationship into greater areas of vulnerability and trust. You're leading through other people by empowering them to interact with you in deeper ways.

These lead to the "1 + 1 = Unlimited" equation that I mentioned in chapter 11 because you've expended the possibilities for more trust. Both of you can now create more together than either of you could alone. I've found you get much more accomplished when two people are involved in the process. I liken it to a passage I've heard read at a number of weddings from Ecclesiastes 4:9–10: "Two are better than one because they have a good return for their labor. For if either of them falls, the one will lift up his companion. But woe to the one who falls when there is not another to lift him up" (NASB).

The second tool I use for building trust is to keep a "must do" list. This is different from a "to do" list. Every Sunday, I make a list of the three things I want to accomplish during the coming week. I write down in precise language what they are, and then I do the same thing the following week, and the week after that, and on and on.

The "must do" list teaches me to focus on what's most important, how to delegate to others, and how to trust them. I learn to not be overinvolved or underinvolved, but to create an environment that allows for just the right amount of engagement from me and for others to take responsibility and thrive. This is how I trust myself to keep my ego in check.

The third and perhaps most important tool related to trust is simply to take complete ownership of the things I've done (or not done). I have to believe this is the equivalent of the "blinding flash of the obvious" to most people, but many times our egos simply get in the way. This is the biggest tool for cleaning up the distrust that we create, because it goes well beyond the typical apology. How often have we heard an apology from a celebrity—a sports star, politician, actor, and so forth—and sensed that it was forced? It's easy to criticize those celebrities, but most of us are guilty of doing the same thing with our friends, coworkers, and family. I know I'm guilty of it.

Taking ownership of what we've done is the difference between a halfhearted and a genuine apology to another person. When we truly own something, we're not just saying, "I'm sorry that happened." We're saying, "What I did not only let you down, but it really let me down. I'm better than that, and here's what I am going to do to address it." We want that other person to trust the sincerity of our apology and for both people to move beyond it and grow from the experience.

I've learned a lot about trust over the years, and the last few years have helped me put the value and power of trust in perspective. I've distilled these into three key truths about trust.

First, there is a connection between trust and joy. When I've been at my best as a father, husband, leader, or friend, trust was always involved.

Second, none of us are invulnerable—and we don't need to be. We just need to show, not tell, others who we truly are and what our core values are, and we need to surround ourselves with people we can lean on and trust. When we have stability and trust in our faith, our family, and our friends, we free up our capacity to think creatively in other areas of life because we don't have to worry about our foundation and core.

Third, balance comes from trusting what we believe in. Clarity comes from trusting ourselves, which creates self-esteem, which in turn creates internal peace and the foundation of a fulfilled life.

Chapter 19

# Marked by Joy

"There are no constraints on the human
mind, no walls around the human spirit,
no barriers to our progress except those
we ourselves erect."

—*Ronald Reagan*

BLUEDOG BROWN lives the good life. He doesn't have a
care in the world, and there's not a part of the world
that he doesn't seem to care about. Drop by my house
sometime, and Bluedog Brown the Black Labrador—or
Blue, for short—will greet you with unconditional love
and affection. Whether you've been here before or this is
your first meeting, he'll treat you as his very best friend.

So perhaps it's fitting that the Labrador who has been
with me through many of my toughest times in life also
was there for one of my biggest "aha!" moments. It was
February 28, 2013, fifteen months after my experience in
New York, and Blue and I were outside my house doing
what he loves most: playing fetch in the twilight of the
day.

I'd toss the tennis ball down the snow-covered grass, and Blue would race at warp speed to retrieve it. Back he'd come, tail wagging, ball in mouth, and joy in his eyes, as this white plume of snow would lightly settle at my feet.

Standing on the snow throwing a ball to Blue that evening, it hit me in a fresh, very real way that my experience in New York had actually turned out to be the best thing that ever happened in my life.

I made some extremely tough decisions following that night in New York, many of them risky and almost all of them leading to some hard changes that I had to make if I ever wanted transformation in my life. In the midst of them, I saw glimmers and even flashes of hope and progress, but there also were times when I backslid into old ways or felt like simply giving up.

I'd love to tell you that those days are over, but, of course, they're not. I still allow dark thoughts into my head. I still make bad decisions. I still have moments of self-doubt. I still feel the pangs of depression.

On this day with Blue, however, instead of dwelling on those setbacks, I kept tossing the ball again and began as I worked my way through a mental checklist of how far I'd really come during the previous fifteen months:

- I had gone through a difficult divorce, but my home life no longer felt in shambles. I now had a new house that felt like mine and that I loved, not for its physical attributes but for the stability I felt of a joy- and peace-filled place that provided solace as I was beginning to envision my life post-marriage.

- I had sold my business, even though it was thriving, because I felt strongly that I needed a fresh start.

Now I was about to start a new job with a team of people that I respected and admired as its President of Business Development.

- I knew who my true friends were and why I could trust them.

- My relationship with God had changed from something transactional to something truly relational.

- I felt good about my role and direction as a father and could see that my relationship with my son was continuing on a very solid path.

- And, finally, there was peace in my heart, because I was beginning to reap the benefits of all the spiritual muscle I was learning to build. I couldn't believe how awesome and blessed my life had become.

I got through that list and I realized that if New York hadn't happened, I'd still be trapped in my same old prisons.

"There are a lot of things I want Tim to accomplish," God seemed to be saying the night He knew I wouldn't jump off that balcony, "and he's not going to accomplish them where his head is right now. I'm going to wake him up."

So here's what I realized as I stood tossing the tennis ball with Blue: My life now is marked by joy rather than the pursuit of happiness. Before, when things didn't feel "right," I would default to depression and respond by pursuing happiness. Now, I realized, my default was joy. I wasn't trying to escape anything. I was motivated to live in that joy.

I started laughing. A joyful laugh. And I just kept laughing and throwing the ball to Bluedog Brown the Black Labrador.

I WAS A HAPPY MAN as I reflected on my life while playing fetch, but my "aha!" moment went deeper than happiness. When a life is marked by joy, that's far greater and far more important than happiness. The feeling of happiness equates to happenings. It's about what's happening in the world at any given moment, about what comes and then goes with the wind. It's dictated by external circumstances. No matter how hard we may try, we can't control the timing of happiness.

Joy comes from inside and exists apart from the happenings of the outside world. When we accept joy as our driver instead of happiness, we come to understand that the occurrences around and within us are nothing more than events. Occurrences evaporate. Events fade and disappear. Joy endures and triumphs.

At some point in life, most of us realize that the things we find most challenging also bring us the most satisfaction. Raising children is incredibly hard and often frustrating, but it's also a constant source of joy. In business, the best projects are arduous and leave us worn out but completely satisfied.

When we're joyful, we welcome the ongoing challenges of life instead of feeling victimized by them. That's because joy comes from cultivating a deep-rooted faith in something bigger than ourselves, and then trusting that the events and circumstances of our lives—good, bad, or in between—don't define us or control us.

Nothing is more draining than trying to maintain control over something we never could control in the first place, but we can waste an enormous amount of effort making the attempt to satisfy false gods. Instead of searching for happiness and finding it, at best, sporadically, we can live in the joy of knowing the unconditional love of God.

If we look for happiness at work, for instance, we very often end up miserable because so many things happen at work that don't make us happy. We don't get the promotion. A client gets angry and pulls business from us. We miss a deadline. A key employee quits during a busy time. Our boss blames us for something we didn't do. We dread another business trip. Our spouse complains that we work too much so we aren't home enough. The list goes on. Soon we find ourselves looking for another job because we're just not happy.

If we look for joy instead and we're willing to contribute to and participate with that joy every day, the right career comes along.

The same is true with dating. I remember in my mid-twenties feeling rejected and not understanding why a woman had broken up with me. I attached too much emotion and self-worth to the outcome, to the external events of the relationship. Then somebody new would come along, and I'd realize how much time I'd wasted trying to appease the other woman or beating myself up because I thought I'd failed in that previous relationship.

There's a direct correlation between the compassion we have for ourselves—that's Self with the capital S—and the joy we're able to create. Being overly hard on myself has mired my whole life. Since the experience at the Bentley Hotel, I've been able to provide an abundance of compassion for others, but I still struggle with how I do that for myself. I view this as the biggest remaining hurdle for me to truly activate the joy inside my soul—loving myself unconditionally as God already does.

I looked for happiness in marriage before realizing that what I truly wanted was joy. Looking back, I'm glad I was married, even though it ended in divorce. There was great value and learning in the experience, and while the temporary happiness and the event of the marriage ended, the joy that it brought stayed with me—often through the eyes of my son.

HAPPINESS AND JOY ARE DIFFERENT. Happiness is a feeling, and feelings are by nature transitory, while joy is a state of being. Happiness appeals to the ego and is therefore temporary. Joy appeals to the selfless side of us and is therefore enduring.

So joy starts by giving thanks for all the things and people in our lives that add value not just to our lives but also to everything around us. That's why the first tool for building joy is to pray ceaselessly. When we pray ceaselessly with gratitude, we are simply recognizing the small things in life that bring joy and observing how over time they compound into bigger things. The ordinary grows into the extraordinary. The daily good habit becomes the monthly gain in joy.

The next tool is to ask ourselves, "What brings me joy?" and then being vigilant about honoring that list. When I search for happiness, I find myself focusing on the things I think are missing in my life. But when I search for joy, I find myself focusing on what I have—especially the good things.

So if we want more joy, we have to identify the things that give us joy and go do those things more often. I've since asked friends who are struggling whether they've ever made a list of what brings them joy. The answer has been overwhelmingly "no," yet they've continued to be focused on business as usual while their giving cup continues to dry up. If we don't understand what brings us joy and makes us light up inside, I struggle with how we're truly able to give back to others and reap the rewards that giving brings back to Self.

Here's a little of what my "brings joy" list looks like:

- Throwing the ball to my dog and seeing how excited he gets.
- Going for a walk.
- Serving others differently.
- Searching for Christmas gifts that are unique, hard to find, and memorable.
- Having conversations just to get to know someone—sharing stories, experiences, vulnerabilities, and realizing how we're connected.
- Working on this book project.
- Spending time with my son and watching him play sports.
- Thinking about the legacy I want to leave . . . realizing there's something out there bigger than me and I still get to be a part of it.
- Being at home.
- Taking photos and looking at great photos others have taken.
- Making a difference in the lives of others who then will make a difference in the lives of others.

I sometimes wonder what would have happened if that CEO hadn't been in the audience to hear my vulnerability. But he was, and we both had the privilege of sharing in one of life's "butterfly effect" moments—that's the theory that a small change in one place can have a huge effect on other things far away because of how the actions are tied together. It's sort of like the Christmas movie *It's a Wonderful Life*, where George sees how the lives of others would have ended up had he not been there.

I believe God uses us for purposes of which we may never know. Yet, when we get glimpses of how we've changed another person's life for the better, it is one of the most powerful and empowering feelings we can experience. It's like a quadruple shot of joy-filled espresso! I hope the many people who have helped me on my journey have felt that joy, and I do my best to tell them—and others—how they've made a difference in my life.

For instance, not long before my up-or-down moment at the Bentley Hotel, I went for a walk with one of my closest friends, Peter Bryant, and he suggested I download a copy of *The Purpose Driven Life*, the best-selling book by Rick Warren. I didn't read it for months, but it was on my iPad during that trip to New York. On the flight home, I read it nonstop and went on to read it cover to cover three times over the next four months. I discovered why it's had such a huge impact on people around the world.

A few months later, I bought two hundred copies of the book and sent them to friends, each with a personal note attached. One copy went to Peter Bryant. "You helped to save my life," I told him. "I wanted you to have a new copy so every time you see it on the shelf you'll think about our walk."

Joy comes from perceiving every moment that we're awake in the world and from grasping that many things—like the relationship that resulted from that speech or the impact of Peter's suggestion of a book—don't happen randomly, but for a reason. I stopped believing in coincidences after New York and continue to be reminded of that new life lesson frequently.

No one can avoid pain, but people who live from a place of joy don't find the pain as disturbing. Why? Because they see pain as a gift and an opportunity to reframe the situation.

We can either dwell in sadness or we can consistently build joy through faith. Those are our two options; there is no third.

THE PEOPLE IN THE PEANUT GALLERY of our lives will always focus on the event of the parade, not on why we've chosen to jump into the parade. They're stalled and stuck and left feeling empty because they can't explain—or even imagine—why we would be full of such joy.

But joy doesn't seek external approval. We can't get joy in life by asking others what joy means. The only place to find joy is within.

And while naysayers try to steal our joy, the right people add to our joy and see us through our darkest times.

At the most critical and gut-wrenching moments of my life, I relied on the things and the people who'd given me joy to get me through. It was my deep-rooted faith in them, not my achievements in the world, that made me begin to see the light. I chose a larger purpose in life.

ONE OF THE MOST CRITICAL CHARACTERISTICS of joy is that it's not linear or limited by time and space. It's unlimited and transcends time, space, and other states of mind and meaning. It gives us a steadiness of purpose and of being that others can sense and feel. There's truly energy in joy.

People won't continue to follow leaders who live in the extremes or who show frustration and self-doubt. They will, however, follow joy. It inspires. It creates. It expands. Joy is contagious.

People who seek happiness are always moving up or down, because the quest for happiness lacks a steady nature. It's hard to follow this leadership style. It's great when we have happiness, but if we're centered on it, we crash emotionally when it dissipates. Happiness can become a drug generated by our minds, an elusive high we can't live without, that we'll do anything—and I mean anything—to get, and yet it doesn't sustain us, so we're always searching for more of it again when the temporary highs are gone.

When we have joy, however, we're givers, not takers, and we're not dependent on the next fix that comes from someone or something else. We're no longer involved in a one-way conversation with ourselves. Instead of being a bystander to passing events, we're a passionate participant in creating and sustaining our own joy.

SINCE I'VE EXCHANGED the pursuit of happiness for building joy, I'm much more at ease with getting out of my comfort zone, in the business world and beyond. Why? Because I'm living into alignment in all my worlds and now it's one big community.

A high state of joy creates a high state of self-esteem. I convey my joy by being interested in others because I don't need to be the center of attention. People who can take the time to do this are coming from an abundance of self-esteem. They can stand back and place the spotlight on others. They've cleaned up their house and aren't chasing the vapor cloud of happiness.

In a state of joy, it's easier to feel vulnerable without feeling afraid of being judged or rejected.

Chapter 20

# The Art of the Comeback: from Victim to Victor

"When you come to a fork in the road, take it."

—*Yogi Berra*

CANCÚN DRAWS TOURISTS from all over the world to its Mayan ruins, Caribbean beaches, and luxurious resorts, so most people don't give much thought to the literal translation of the city's name: *Nest of snakes*.

That name turned out to be true. I didn't encounter any real snakes when I visited Cancún in October 2013, but, metaphorically, I found myself in a nest full of them.

On the surface, it looked like the perfect getaway. I was there on business, and what better place to go for "work" than a resort in Mexico? Instead of lounging in the lap of luxury, however, I fell into an all-too-familiar nest.

It was my first solo trip abroad since my late twenties, so I was experiencing some isolation. As I said earlier, I don't like to fly, nor do I have particularly good memories of hotels or business travel (you know, that whole Bentley thing). On top of that, I wouldn't be just "one of the guys" at the conference. I was making a keynote address on business performance to a group of nearly two hundred franchise owners, so I was the one everyone was supposed to look up to. Paired with the feelings of loneliness was a nervousness about making what was to be my first major corporate keynote address. Fears of inadequacy filled me. Would I say the right thing? Was I really successful enough to have such a platform? What if I gave a bad speech and disappointed the owner of the company—a friend who had hired me for the event?

It wasn't long before I was combatting thoughts similar to those that had attacked me that night in New York. I let my thoughts drift to places that were unhealthy, and I lost focus on the positives in my life. I felt weak. I even had physical shakes similar to the ones I had experienced that night in New York. Scary, to say the least.

It was one of my worst days since that night in New York, but it also quickly became a gift because I learned that God was offering me a chance to live into alignment and seek clarity and joy while serving others. Instead of continuing down that dark path of despair, I stopped and channeled what I was experiencing into expressions of gratitude and trust in something more powerful than myself.

What helped me get to that point were some encouraging words from my friend Laura, first through a text message, then a phone call, and finally through an email she wrote. Laura is a woman I've known in professional circles for more than a decade, but before the trip we had been rekindling and deepening our friendship. She wasn't in Mexico, but shortly after I arrived I reached out to her about the struggle I was facing.

I believe God used Laura to help me refocus and turn the corner back toward peace and joy.

The email she sent in response let me know I wasn't alone, that someone really understood my battle and was there for me when I needed it. Here's part of what she wrote:

"I trust that you will feel your way through this. I also believe that you may look at this trip as something that could be the beginning of the new way you travel for business . . . as opposed to a remnant of the old. This time it is to share wisdom, serve others, and leave people wanting more from you as a person, not as a company. Try to look at this as a reset on your vision for your life."

While the email encouraged me, and helped me not feel so alone, I continued to fight an inner battle where the smallest of negative thoughts became boulders. When Laura and I talked on the phone that night, she asked me to describe what was wrong. Then she switched gears in a very powerful way by asking me what was going right in my life.

I began to list them in no particular order: I have clarity around how I want to live my life . . . I'm secure in my relationship with God . . . I'm confident in my ability to overcome certain fears . . . My son is healthy . . . I am healthy . . . I understand who my real friends are . . . I'm developing relationships with those friends at even deeper levels . . .

As I talked through that list of positives with her, the fog of uneasiness began to lift. The snakes began to slither away, back into their hiding holes, as if they now realized they had no chance to cause harm. Within ten minutes I had a completely different mind-set, and I went on to deliver a very powerful keynote speech the next morning.

When I look back on that trip, I realize that I had used many, if not all, of the skills I've been sharing in this book, and I had used them in real time. There was no one to "save me" except God. I prayed for Christ to fill my heart with His light and peace, and He did so—working through Laura and opening my heart to other insights that allowed me to survive and thrive.

I learned something valuable about myself from the experience, something I hold onto as I face new challenges each day: When the inevitable storms of life hit me, I can go from victim to victor.

THE BEST PHRASE I'VE HEARD to describe the process that's helped me move from victim to victor came from a friend I first met in business and became reacquainted with in my late thirties when we happened to be in the same group that was training for IRONMAN events.

Kirk MacDonald, a former CEO in the newspaper industry, has faced and overcome many challenges in his life, including a failed business venture and a bout with cancer. Through it all, he's shown great class, character, and resilience. What he learned in his business failure, he has applied to his own comeback in the form of a highly successful digital ad network, now in 133 cities and six countries worldwide.

One day, while the two of us were out on a fast-paced bike-training ride, I was lamenting the loss of the radio stations, and Kirk turned to me and delivered the succinct, timely wisdom for which he's become known: "You keep looking in the rearview mirror and not looking ahead," he said. "Life is all about the art of the comeback."

Donald Trump used that phrase as the title of a book about bouncing back in business, but the art of the comeback is much bigger than business. It's about life. It's about moving from victim to victor—each day, every day.

My trip to Cancún served as a powerful reminder of the lessons I'm learning about successfully making my personal comeback—lessons I've been sharing throughout this book. So I'd like to hit on a few of them one last time, because I believe they apply to all of us.

First, a comeback begins with a simple, conscious step in whatever direction we want to go, but we have to commit to it and use our values to guide us.

Our values are a commitment algorithm. When the values are false, the algorithm produces false answers, just as with any mathematical equation. When the values are truly our own, the algorithm produces the answer and the truth within us.

When I was growing up, we checked our work in long division by multiplying the answer times the denominator to arrive at the numerator. If we want to check our "work" in life, we can use the values algorithm. For example, if we value honesty, is what we're doing in our lives in alignment with that? Again, as Senator Moynihan said, "We can have our own opinions, but we can't have our own facts." Are the facts about our values lining up with our words? The values, just like the numbers, never lie.

In business, if companies don't use the right numbers, people go to prison, corporations fail, and stockholders lose money—all because the equations never could add up to the truth. Life isn't any different. We can't cheat the system. Making a comeback takes a commitment to True North. It's the only way we create a genuine transformation so that we can jump into the parade.

Second, the transformation starts with shifting perspective and focusing on what is going right in your life.

We have to focus on what's working in life and be willing to let the rest go. When we focus on the right things— serving others, defining and living into our values, living for something bigger than ourselves—we begin to see ourselves as participants in life and not victims of life. We learn from where we've been, but we see where we are and where we're going.

This forward focus creates momentum. It starts off slowly, but the momentum compounds with each new day of doing the same things until what once was ordinary in life becomes extraordinary.

We move forward by putting God first, others second, and ourselves third. Then we remake this commitment throughout each day.

Third, not every day is going to feel good, so the art of the comeback requires patience with ourselves and others and a long-term view of our journey. Comebacks take time and effort. Building spiritual muscle is like losing weight—we don't add weight overnight and we can't lose it in a matter of days. We have to patiently and persistently push through the hard days.

It also takes hard work to maintain muscle. A muscle, physical or spiritual, is only as strong as the last time it was used. Without exercise, it quickly becomes flabby. So, again, living in alignment is something we have to recommit to every day.

The truth is, life sometimes kicks us in the teeth. Sometimes reality lands a sucker punch that we never saw coming. (Okay, this isn't completely true; most of the time, we see it coming, but choose to turn our heads and ignore it until we feel the pain.)

As we experience the art of the comeback, our problems don't magically go away, but we are given a different framework from which to view life. We begin to recognize that pain is a part of marriage and business and raising children and confronting our selfish selves. It's part of life. It's a part of the journey, and it happens to all of us. The art of the comeback is about using that pain to move from victim to victor.

The fourth part of the art of the comeback relates to the power of forgiveness and acceptance. It hit me hard on that trip that the line I had drawn between my old life and my new life had not disconnected them. I needed to love, embrace, and accept all of it—and all of me. I had to forgive myself for things that happened in the past in order to embrace all of me. In Mexico, I let the old me use the old self-berating tactics with the new me, and it caused quite a clash. By forgiving, accepting, loving, and truly *embracing* all of me, I made a quantum step forward in healing. I could understand it in my head and feel it in my heart.

We're all human, and we all make mistakes. God loves us despite our mistakes, and we need to give the same grace to others and ourselves. For me, that meant letting go of the venom I carried around inside of me from child-hood and that I created as an adult. It affected everything I did. When I finally just forgave it, all of it, and got rid of it, it felt great. As a friend of mine used to tell me, "You know, Tim, when you've got a hammer in your right hand and you keep banging it against your head over and over again, it feels really good when you stop."

The only thing we need to bring forward from our past is the wisdom we've collected and the experiences we've learned from. We have to willingly—sometimes forcefully—cut ties with the old pain, the old baggage, and the old issues.

Finally, there is value in comeback stories. The world is full of stories of people who have taken advantage of second chances to turn their lives around. Living one of those stories produces vitality, and vitality takes us out of just existing and into living fully—that's when we're truly jumping into the parade.

It's empowering to know others might look at us and say, "If he can fall down, but come back like that, I can, too. And maybe I can inspire others to get through something difficult with their lives and transform themselves."

The only way to create inspiration is by sharing our life path with others. The stories are rarely pretty, but they always inspire. We're all connected. Take a chance to create inspiration.

IN ADDITION TO SHARING YOUR LIFE in general, it's important to invest in friendships and relationships where you're more focused on serving than in being served. It is good for both you and others.

A friend of mine passed along a study that showed people with close friendships tended to have fewer illnesses and lower stress. Life is clearly more stressful for people who struggle to make friends. And we all know that stress can have severe consequences: hypertension, headaches, and depression, among other things. The interaction and support of close friends helps us feel better. We actually feel pleasure, and that's a rewarding experience for our brains, and our souls.

There's also an internal thrill from serving others. During my Half IRONMAN races, I experienced the euphoria you get from running (the "runner's high"). It is purely physical and always temporary; however, the rush we get from giving to others—the "giver's high"—is always permanent. When we serve others, we create an endorphin release that creates joy deep inside ourselves. It makes us want to give more because it makes us feel great, and because we see what it does for someone else. If you don't believe this, take the giver's-high challenge: Try giving for twenty-one straight days and see how you feel.

LIKE SO MANY OF US, I was once extremely adept at creating a façade of success, prosperity, and well-being. Behind the façade, I was ensnarled in conflict and adversity. When I became clear about my own truths, I was able to fully jump into the parade again. This time it just happened to be my parade.

As often happens in so many stories, I came to the ubiquitous fork in the road and found two very different paths.

Turning left meant continuing to do exactly as I'd done since reaching adulthood; it meant that no matter how much success I achieved in the outside world, I still held only my role as a victim within. Turning left would mean I would not be in control but that I would try to control everything. With that path, I would keep trying to force appeasement and integrity together, even though I had learned the hard way that those two things can never coexist.

Instead, I turned right.

This meant stepping into what was for me completely unknown, untried, and untested. It meant giving up the notion that I was supposed to have the answers. It meant traveling down a path that offered ten times the choices, even though some of them were hidden. It meant giving up my old definitions and illusions about success and having a much clearer vision of what would become my highest priorities in life: my faith, family, and friends (my "three F's").

Turning right required a new focus and creating a new identity. Instead of the victim's mentality, it meant placing a new emphasis on becoming victorious.

Turning right meant taking the harder but better road—or, as a wise man once said, "The only way out of it is through it."

The choice I made that night in New York liberated me. Instead of allowing myself to remain shackled, I jumped into the parade of life. And so rather than providing the marker for the end, my day of reckoning now marks a rebirth. With this second chance, I'm now living a life that, while not perfect, is full of joy. It's a joy that isn't based on wealth and prestige, but on faith, family, and friends—and always in that order. I have learned that the only way to fully experience joy is in the present. So today I am following my heart and pursuing opportunities in life that connect with my passions and values.

The last few years of my life have been a challenge both personally and professionally. But when I reframe my own experiences, I realize I am a better person, a better parent, a better friend, a better partner, and a better business leader. It's given me a firmer grip on my integrity and a better focus on my purpose in the world. I can't say for certain where I'm going to go from here, but I can say that I'm never going back to the past.

Every day I make a new commitment to the present and the future—and to serving others more intently. And with that forward commitment comes an acknowledgment of my past. When I began writing this book, I divided my life into the "old me" and the "new me." I've come to learn that the old life is just as important as my new life. I've learned to embrace all parts of my life—the old for the perspective and lessons it provided and the new for the experiences yet to come.

For me, the transformative part of the journey was about the rediscovery of my integrity and my deeper connections to what I am as a human being. I didn't have to invent anything new to accomplish this; I simply needed to join with what was already there. When the student was ready for change, the teacher was there waiting. He'd been there all along.

Conclusion

# Broken? Who, Me?

> "There's beauty in imperfection. When
> something becomes too polished, it
> loses its soul."
>
> —*Christine Caine, author, speaker, and*
> *cofounder of the A21 Campaign*

WAS IN A ROOM FULL OF MY PEERS, more than a hundred men and women who also were presidents and leaders of their multimillion-dollar organizations, and we had been assigned a task that would put our collective brokenness on display. We all took note cards and, without including our names, wrote down at least two of our "darkest secrets." We turned the cards in and the moderator read each one aloud to the group.

This was the cream of the Colorado business world crop—highly energetic, highly competitive, highly successful—and yet our cards told another story. The cards told of men and women who were broken. Worse, many of us were trapped in our brokenness, trapped in our guilt, trapped in the self-perceived shame of our imperfections.

Some were involved in affairs and in danger of losing their families. Others were on the brink of personal bankruptcy, living paycheck to paycheck and juggling large living expenses to keep up appearances. Others faced the looming collapse of their businesses. Some were fighting different forms of depression or battling addictions to drugs, alcohol, or pornography. Others were dealing with things largely out of their control—destructive choices made by spouses or children.

The cards didn't lack variety or spice.

I put my head into my hands for several seconds as I listened, and then I turned to a close friend who was sitting next to me.

"Can you believe we're this messed up?" I asked.

"Yes," he said with an even tone. "We're all broken."

*And, yet,* I thought, *we hide it so well.*

Brokenness is one of life's great equalizers. Money can't buy happiness and it sure can't buy joy, but people with resources typically hide their brokenness—at least temporarily. It doesn't stay hidden forever, however. It eventually comes out, as it did for me. It's like a cork in water—you can push it down, but it inevitably resurfaces. Brokenness emanates from a variety of dark places— pride, greed, lack of self-esteem, selfish ambition, failure, arrogance, insecurity—all of which are rooted in fear that keeps us trapped from living the life we were created to live. And no matter where we live or how much money, fame, or success we have (or believe we have), brokenness makes a home within all of us—until we do something about it. Even then, we're still broken, but we're on the road to something far better in life, and our awareness of it means we can make it work for us instead of against us.

So if we're all imperfectly perfect, why not embrace it? Why not shout for joy and wear it like a badge of honor? Read almost any self-help book and you'll spot a common theme: *You are broken and this book will help fix you.* Here's a different idea: *You're broken? Welcome to the club, buddy. Let's help each other deal with our brokenness, improve where we can, and live with joy despite our imperfections.*

This book showed how I came crashing into my own brokenness and began the painful process of deconstructing and reconstructing my life. The lessons you've read about are applicable to anyone in any state of brokenness, even those who think they aren't really broken.

The lessons are best described in the business world as "life leadership" lessons because they benefit our lives as a whole, not just in this segment or that segment. Brokenness, I've discovered, isn't something we check at the door as we move from one room of our life to another. If we're struggling at work, we'll take those struggles home to our family. If we're struggling in our personal life, we'll take those struggles to work. If our spiritual life is weak, the kinks will show up in all our relationships. Our brokenness is a by-product of our pasts, our circumstances, and our relationships, and it's a reflection of all of who we are, not just one part.

Mine is a story of severe brokenness, or so it felt—and still sometimes feels. But that's not the point. A cracked glass holds no more water than a glass that's shattered; it just leaks at a different pace. Everyone's brokenness is personal and severe in its own way. So the point isn't to compare brokenness, but to acknowledge and deal with it. And we *can* deal with it. We can turn it around and use it for our empowerment.

That's the real point.

If depression has become your drug, pulling you down a path to the shadow lands, take heart. There's hope. "Depression" need only exist in language; it doesn't have to be your reality. If you're feeling pretty good about life and simply have to deal with the inevitable storms that blow in from time to time, take heart. There's hope. Those storms always end, and—at the risk of sounding too Pollyannaish—sunny days always follow the storms.

I can say that because for me, the lowest point in my life—the point of my greatest suffering—turned out to be the best thing that could have happened to me. Suffering led me to something great: a transformed life. Dave Zobl, a friend of mine and one of the many who helped me through my journey, put it this way: "Sometimes you have to go into a dark room to expose a great picture. You're in a tough time and it's dark. When you come out, there will be so many colors you won't know what to do."

I was amazed to later discover how suffering connects us all and makes us feel more human—more imperfectly perfect. In the Club of the Broken, we go through dark times, but there's always hope, and my story illustrates where this hope leads: to an imperfect life that's marked by joy and contentment regardless of the circumstances. Your results may vary, as the advertisers say, but I am someone who went from extreme depression to one who learned to jump into the parade and live with more wholeness and purity of purpose as a father, friend, business leader, and man of faith. I lived with a purpose before, but it typically wasn't "pure." It was diluted because it was shaped by others or by my perceptions of what others thought, rather than by what was true and best for me.

WE HAVE SEVERAL OPTIONS in our life journey. One, we can sit on the sidelines and watch. We might applaud and encourage others, but we don't get directly involved. If you've ever led a change-management project, you know the importance of getting buy-in from everyone who is affected by the change. You need them to believe in the change—to literally "create" the change, because as humans we're at our best when we're creating. Those who don't approach the work with passion are much like the guy who gives two weeks' notice and then coasts his way out the door. Some of us go through life that way. We don't make waves. We don't actively destroy our work or the works of others. But we're passive rather than proactive about life. This is the safe spot, the spot that requires no commitment and no risk, and brings very limited rewards.

Two, we can chase what the world defines as success. In other words, our vision and purpose are defined by others—perhaps our work culture or the norms of the neighborhood. We are not directed by a mission that is tied to who we uniquely are. Many of us follow the beaten path, so to speak, because we want to prove we belong, and living up to the expectations of others, real or perceived, provides a sense of control. We're likely motivated by guilt, pride, avarice, or appeasement. We take risks, commit to ideas and projects, and we do win, but it's always on a surface level. We lack contentment at our cores. Something is gnawing at our souls, and the victories feel as empty as a bird's nest in December.

Three, we can jump into the parade, grounded in a sense of who we are, what we believe, and where we want to go. This means we bring passion to the table, take risks, and commit to ideas and projects not because we are trying to be successful on someone else's terms, but because we are committed to ourselves and to a higher calling. We are taking the road we feel is best for us, not necessarily the one our peers are traveling down. And while this path may have bumps, sharp turns, and dark alleys at times, there is joy on it because we've embraced that life is to be celebrated. Like a parade, it has cheerfulness built into its nature as well as purpose: It is heading somewhere.

When we identify and own our values, we can create a journey that matters, a parade in which we lead, even if we're not in a traditional position of leadership. If we embody the qualities of a true leader, everybody is watching us, no matter our title. So we're always in a position of influence. We can lead and live a life that has meaning for us and makes a meaningful difference in the lives of the community around us, because we're testifying to how we're not as broken as we used to be and how our new appetite for life has come through living in alignment with our core values.

If we jump into the parade, we will change on the inside, but it will also affect the things we do on the outside. It means getting our hands dirty, embracing change, taking risks, and loving the world—through action. Jumping into the parade allows us to contribute to the greater good, kick-start a movement, launch a business, take a relationship to the next level, make a difference in someone's life, or pursue a dream. It means loving God, loving our family, loving our friends, and loving ourselves.

Our world is littered with stories of people who saw an opportunity and, paralyzed by fear, watched that opportunity pass them by. Others seize opportunities but, trapped by fear, abandon their personal values and end up miserable because even the good things were done for all the wrong reasons. In short, their "success" is actually failure.

We all have the power to help shape our outcomes in life, to move from reactive to proactive and passionately create the results we want in life. As my former father-in-law once told me, "Very few really good and valuable things happen in this world without someone, or most likely a collection of someones, making it happen."

I have spent most of my life "making it happen," but for many of the wrong reasons. I was trapped in my brokenness. Regardless of whether I was a child living in a seemingly run-down apartment in south Florida or an adult living with my family in a multimillion-dollar home in Denver, I was broken. I literally could recite my rags-to-riches narrative while my brokenness came along for the ride. Well, more accurately, it drove most of the way.

It took me more than forty years to free myself from that trap, and I very nearly died in the process. But then I made a different choice: I chose gratitude, and I jumped into the parade.

# Tim's 13:
# Jumping into Your Own Parade

> "Set goals so big that unless God helps you, you will be a miserable failure."
>
> —Bill Bright

IN LOUISIANA, they call it a *lagniappe*—a little something extra. And that's what this section is, a little something extra to the story. It is composed of pieces of advice you can reference quickly to help you remember, retain, and—I hope—put to use some of the lessons I've learned and that I've woven into the book in the telling of my journey. These thirteen aphorisms may make it easier for you to jump into your own parade.

**1. Give up control:** When I gave up the illusion that I was in control of things, the greatest feeling of freedom and peace came over me. I left behind my illusions, I acknowledged my dependence, I surrendered to something much larger than myself, and I committed to jumping into the parade. The heart (led by faith, not by shifting emotions) was in control now, not the head, and that made so much more possible. The heart was ready to look back on—and to feel—what the head had spent decades running from.

**2. Walk in confident humility:** What at first seemed like the worst moment of my life turned out to be the best, because I finally decided to stop being a victim and to move toward something new. This "something new" included a shift away from serving my ego, an acknowledgment that I don't have all the answers, and a willingness to submit my life to a higher power. As my humility increased, my world expanded. This was, and remains, an incredible process.

**3. Don't fear your fear:** "False Expectations Appearing Real"—that's the spelling of the acronym FEAR that several people have shared with me. A thought or a feeling may seem very real at the time it comes to you, but 99 percent of all the things we're afraid of never occur. We spend our lives inside of fears we have built and nurtured from our earliest and most unconscious days. The moment we realize we have at least one other choice, we are no longer trapped.

   None of us like getting out of our comfort zones, but that's where most of our growth occurs. When we go there, the experience controls what happens next, not us. I only changed because of the presence of so many negative feelings, not positive feelings . . . and I learned that fear is just the absence of courage.

**4. Stick with the process:** I thought I had buried all my lies at the bottom of the Grand Canyon, but within a year I had realized that it was only a start. A good start, but still just a start. It served a very real purpose at the time, but I came to understand that burying the lies is a process that takes time. I suspect I've buried about 50 percent of my lies (best case). It's part of the journey, and all the more reason why we have to recommit each day to believing that we're worthy of grace, love, and acceptance.

**5. Value your past:** I continue to understand and deeply value how my background has come to serve me in developing my life perspective, my service to others, and in understanding my core values. We have the power to reframe and turn adversity into life opportunities, and I remind myself of that daily.

**6. Find your place:** The big "S" of selflessness is a place, not some concept or abstract state that you casually glaze over while sitting in church. You can't run and hide in this place, but in this place you get back tenfold whatever you contribute. It requires effort, almost like tithing but with "spiritual capital," not money. It requires that you genuinely think about others and pay it forward.

**7. Listen up:** There's a very good reason why God gave us two ears and only one mouth. When we use an open heart that seeks answers by asking twice as many questions as statements, that's the big "S" in action . . .

**8. Have a vigilant heart:** The world of head knowledge is filled with conflict and gray areas. In the realm of heart wisdom, you have clarity of purpose without the burden of all that uncertainty and gray. By being vigilant to the heart, you have access to more tools. You can trust your belief system and understand what your values are and why you value them. You can stay close enough to God to trust that your inner voice is His way of speaking to you. (Warning: If you don't stay close to Him, then that voice isn't His.) By using those tools in a sustained way, you gain even more access to the wisdom of the heart. It's a closed loop of endless expansion. This not only makes you more effective as a leader in the present, but also will make your future and your legacy have far more of an impact.

**9. Learn from your experiences:** It's only called wisdom if we learn something from our experiences. Make the dash between your years represent the time you spent clarifying what you wanted from life and then pursuing it without fear.

**10. Stop "shoulding":** Most victimization is self-victimization. Most of what we hear in our heads about what we should be doing came from somebody else long ago. Many of us don't even know what exists outside the "shoulds"—I *should* take this job, I *should* live in this neighborhood, I *should* join this club—because we haven't taken the time or had the discipline to explore the questions. You have the right to stop "shoulding" on yourself, but only you have the power to do it.

**11. Refocus your thoughts:** Show me a person who is focused on problems, and I'll show you a person who has lots of problems in his or her life. The opposite is equally true. When we focus on the positive things in life, we feel better about life. If you're on a diet, you can focus on the fact that you can't eat a cheeseburger and fries, or you can focus on how much you like the fish you'll have for dinner. You can focus on the fact that you only lost three pounds during the week or you can celebrate that you lost three pounds during the week.

**12. Share your life:** Showing vulnerability builds trust faster than anything else. The opposite of being vulnerable is being closed, guarded, or sheltered, where it's difficult to trust, or where people find you to be above them or aloof. When we open up about the positive and negative experiences of our lives, others relate to those experiences and trust us more. We don't have to say everything we think and feel to everyone we know, but most of us can open up more and move beyond surface-level topics like the weather, sports, or the news.

**13. Get yourself some joy:** The best thing any of us can do for ourselves is give up the hunt for happiness and make a genuine commitment to finding joy. Remember, happiness is tied to the external circumstances of our lives, and we can't control those circumstances. Joy resides within us and isn't driven by circumstances. Until we embrace joy as the driver in our lives, our words will be empty, our prayers will fall flat, and our actions won't be nearly as productive as they could be. Joy comes from the heart and is stable in ways that happiness will never be. So empower an outcome. Create your own day. Make your own experiences. *Carpe diem*. You pick the cliché you like the best, so long as it leads to this: discovering joy.

IF YOU ARE THE ONE PERSON I hoped to reach with this book, then I have succeeded. Know I am here for you

24/7—in spirit, and, if our paths cross, in person. I look forward to witnessing you jumping into your own parade.

*Please feel free to share your own story of "Jumping into the Parade" with me at www.jumpingintotheparade.com.*

# Acknowledgments

GOD SENDS PEOPLE INTO YOUR LIFE for a reason. When I reflect back on the number of people responsible for *Jumping into the Parade*, it is an incredible and humbling list of family members, friends, and colleagues. Every word is the product of the time, attention, and mentorship that people offered to me over the years. I have been especially blessed these past three years with many who served me so authentically by providing their unwavering support during my journey on a new and unfamiliar path to healing, reframing the events of my life, and embracing a new way of being.

As a first-time author, I was not fully prepared for the challenges and deep-soul work required during this process. Saying that I underestimated what it would take would be, well, a major underestimation. Authoring this book made me feel so alive, kept me authentic, and allowed me to live into an experience like never before.

Thank you to all who have been, and continue to be, my rock. Whether it was during countless conversations over coffee, church services, walks, emails, texts, hikes, airplane flights, bike rides, boat rides, car rides, and baseball games, your friendship made a difference. Simply put, we are all connected, and without your support I would have never been able to offer others what has arguably been the toughest project of my life.

A special thanks to:

My son, for your joy, laughter, kindness, and belief that anything is possible.

Phil Anschutz for your patience, love, and grace, and for showing me how to be a life leader through your own actions.

Stephen McGhee for your tough love, countless hours of direction, and helping me understand the power of living inside my integrity.

Laura Love for showing me how to embrace and love all of my life, for being comfortable in your own skin, and illustrating how deeply rich life can be when we learn to reframe our experiences and genuinely welcome joy into our hearts.

Dan Scherer for your vigilance to why faith, family, and friends are the center of life.

Chip Flaherty for being my "guidance counselor" and dispenser of wisdom throughout the entire book-writing process.

John C. Greenwood for never wavering on our friendship and sticking it out with me through the thick and thin.

Stephen Caldwell for all the time we spent together creating the words, paragraphs, and chapters of *Jumping into the Parade.* Your attention to detail, years of writing experience, and thoughtfulness were a shining light.

Tommy Spaulding for your love of others, love of God, and for all the guidance and encouragement you gave me throughout the writing and editorial process.

Peter Bryant for your clarity, reassuring advice, and your constant reminders to pray and turn it over to God.

Kirstin Rowe for helping me understand how incredible and peaceful it feels to know that we're all imperfectly perfect and deserving of God's love.

My YPO Forum, "El Ocho" (Wil Armstrong, Matt Briger, Paul Ford, Byron Haselden, Corbin West, Ken Salazar, and Mike Davis), for the moral support to follow my heart.

Everyone at BenBella Books who made this endeavor possible, especially my publisher, Glenn Yeffeth, for believing in me and my story, and my editor, Debbie Harmsen, who challenged and encouraged me while working countless late nights and weekends, and truly left nothing on the table in terms of effort expended on my behalf.

Lastly, thank you to all of you who took the time to read *Jumping into the Parade.* We're all connected, deserve joy, and have a wonderful life waiting for us to embrace and love. I am grateful for your interest and time invested in learning more about my story. I wish you many blessings on your own story as it continues to be written.